D0805906

The Quotable Kierkegaard

THE QUOTABLE
KIERKEGAARD

Edited by Gordon Marino

PRINCETON UNIVERSITY PRESS
PRINCETON AND OXFORD

Copyright © 2014 by Gordon Marino

Requests for permission to reproduce material from this work should be sent to
Permissions, Princeton University Press

Published by Princeton University Press, 41 William Street, Princeton, New Jersey
08540

In the United Kingdom: Princeton University Press, 6 Oxford Street, Woodstock,
Oxfordshire OX20 1TW

press.princeton.edu

Library of Congress Cataloging-in-Publication Data

Kierkegaard, Søren, 1813–1855.
[Works. Selections. English. 2013]
The quotable Kierkegaard / edited by Gordon Marino.
pages cm
Includes bibliographical references and index.
Summary: "Why I so much prefer autumn to spring is that in the autumn one looks
at heaven—in the spring at the earth."—Søren Kierkegaard. The father of existentialism, Søren Kierkegaard (1813–1855) was a philosopher who could write like an
angel. With only a sentence or two, he could plumb the depths of the human spirit.
In this collection of some 800 quotations, the reader will find dazzling bon mots next
to words of life-changing power. Drawing from the authoritative Princeton editions
of Kierkegaard's writings, this book presents a broad selection of his wit and wisdom,
as well as a stimulating introduction to his life and work. Organized by topic, this
volume covers notable Kierkegaardian concerns such as anxiety, despair, existence,
irony, and the absurd, but also erotic love, the press, busyness, and the comic. Here
readers will encounter both well-known quotations ("Life must be understood backward. But then one forgets the other principle, that it must be lived forward") and
obscure ones ("Beware false prophets who come to you in wolves' clothing but inwardly are sheep—i.e., the phrasemongers"). Those who spend time in these pages
will discover the writer who said, "my grief is my castle," but who also taught that
"the best defense against hypocrisy is love." Illuminating and delightful, this engag-
ing book also provides a substantial portrait of one of the most influential of modern
thinkers. Gathers some 800 quotations Drawn from the authoritative Princeton editions of Kierkegaard's writings Includes an introduction, a brief account and time-
line of Kierkegaard's life, a guide to further reading, and an index"— Provided by
publisher.

ISBN 978-0-691-15530-2 (hardback)
1. Kierkegaard, Søren, 1813–1855—Quotations. I. Marino,
Gordon Daniel, 1952–   II. Title.
B4372.E5 2013
198'.9—dc23

2013034354p4

British Library Cataloging-in-Publication Data is available

This book has been composed in Minion Pro and Trade Gothic

Printed on acid-free paper. ∞

Printed in the United States of America

1 3 5 7 9 10 8 6 4 2

This book is dedicated to my beloved sons, Paul and Philip.
May tenderness and conviction continue to steer your lives.

CONTENTS

ACKNOWLEDGMENTS

Kierkegaard scholars from around the globe and at all different stages of their careers have been so generous in passing along their favorite quotes that this collection could almost be reckoned a group project. I am grateful to these scholars not only for the lines that they have sent me, but even more so for their willingness to reveal where the heart of their interest in the master lies. After all, such revelations are self-revelations.

I am also eager to express my gratitude to the two anonymous reviewers of the text. As a result of their sparkling erudition, I was safeguarded from a number of pitfalls and my introductory essay is stronger than it would have been without their generous advice.

Paul Muench and Peder Garnass-Halvorson, former student workers in the Hong Kierkegaard Library, were very helpful in tracking down obscure quotes. Sonja Gleason-Wermager deserves special thanks for the many hours she devoted to the exacting work of checking texts. Thanks are also due to Seth Thomas for his careful reading of the text. Finally, I have profited and am grateful for the wisdom of Willis Regier, author of *Quotology*.

This humble offering would not have been possible were it not for the steady and insightful guidance of my editor, Rob Tempio. I am also obliged to Ryan Mulligan for his many and noble efforts in shaping this volume.

Finally, my eternal gratitude goes out to my wife, Dr. Susan Marino. Night after night, she gracefully put aside her own research as a neuroscientist to ponder and compare lines from the Danish writer who could make thoughts dance. If Kierkegaard had not taught me otherwise, I would have to think that Susan's love was proof of grace divine.

INTRODUCTION

Though he very rarely characterized himself as a philosopher, that is how world history remembers Søren Aabye Kierkegaard. And yet, while Socrates was his sage and he profoundly respected Kant, Kierkegaard ultimately became a virulent critic of philosophy, especially of the academic ilk. G.W.F Hegel was the regnant philosopher king of early to mid-nineteenth-century European philosophy. While Kierkegaard, in his early career, admired the speculative German thinker, he ultimately concluded that Hegel and other intellectual system builders "are like a man who has built a vast palace while he himself lives next door." Writing in his journal, Kierkegaard insists, "Spiritually, a man's thoughts must be the building in which he lives—otherwise it is wrong" (JN, vol. 2, Journal JJ: 490, p. 279). In addition to being unable to bring their scholarly studies to quotidian life, Kierkegaard complained that philosophers neglected the question of how to communicate the wisdom that philosophers (lovers of wisdom) are supposed to care about and ultimately possess.

Plato wrestled with the question of whether or not the written word was an aid or an impediment to the good and just life, but for the most part the focus in philosophy has always been on *the what*, on the content of thought, as though wisdom in life were a mere matter of information capable of being directly disseminated en masse. With their emphasis on reason, Hegel and other virtuosi of abstractions spent little time pondering *how* it would be best to communicate their conclusions. Indeed, philosophers can seem almost narcissistic in their indifference to the subjective coordinates of their readers. They reason through an issue, such as "What is love?" and then publish the argument, usually in a treatise form accessible only to the likes of philosophy professors.

Unlike other members of the Socrates guild, Kierkegaard grappled with the question of the *how*, as opposed to the *what*, of communication. Someone with an epistemological interest might conclude that while most philosophers probe the question of knowledge, Kierkegaard made a study of belief; Kierkegaard, however, was concerned with more than nodding intellectual assent.

As he wrote in the first few pages of his writing life, Kierkegaard sought a truth that he could live and die by—one to which he could mold his everyday existence. Ordinarily, we think of truth in terms of ideas expressing or reflecting reality. Kierkegaard's thinking, at least on matters moral and religious, moved along a different vector; he prodded himself and his reader to represent ideas in the medium of actions. On his analysis (hoping the reader will forgive the colloquialism) when we fail to walk our talk we literally fail to grasp what we are talking about.

Kierkegaard maintained that a good deal of what goes for communication is chatter, lines we have memorized, ideas that have not been appropriated, as in "The women come and go. Talking of Michael Angelo." It was not just spouting clichés that Kierkegaard railed against, it was the spiritlessness that was given voice in palaver without inwardness. He observed, "Spiritlessness can say exactly the same thing that the richest spirit has said, but it does not say it by virtue of spirit. Man qualified as spiritless has become a talking machine, and there is nothing to prevent him from repeating by rote a philosophical rigmarole, a confession of faith, or a political recitative" (CA, p. 95).

The inwardness that renders our talk something more than talk was the exotic bull's-eye of Kierkegaard's thinking. Like the efforts of a strange meditation teacher, it was as though all of Kierkegaard's writings were directed toward cultivating a certain sort of subjectivity. Sometimes Kierkegaard's prized inner state was described as inwardness, subjectivity, or faith, but more often than not, it was called "earnestness." Of course, there are no direct outward manifestations of this mind/soul set. Earnestness can take a multiplicity of forms depending on the situation and circumstances. In our own "present age" it is an alien concept; mention earnestness and students will often cock their heads puppylike in puzzlement. Perhaps it is closest to "character," but there is more to earnestness than being strong willed, upright, and master of your desires.

Though we delight in his psychological epiphanies, Kierkegaard could be considered an anathema to our happiness/self-fulfillment-obsessed age. He urges us to understand that to a large extent happiness is a matter of fortune. It is something that Kierkegaard believed could happen more or less "as a matter of course," and Kierkegaard was firm that, regarding the development of the spirit, nothing happens "as a matter of course." Twisted as it might seem, Kierkegaard thanked his almost perversely difficult father for ruining his prospects for happiness and yet preparing him for faith. In his lapidary *The Sickness Unto Death*, Kierkegaard wagged his finger, referring to the hiddenness of despair. He writes,

> [H]appiness is not a qualification of spirit, and deep, deep within the most secret hiding place of happiness there dwells also anxiety, which is despair; it very much wishes to be allowed to remain there, because for despair the most cherished and desirable place to live is in the heart of happiness. (SUD, p. 25)

Like Luther, with whom he was always grappling, the Lutheran Kierkegaard thought in terms of the two worlds, this one and the world of the spirit. In this realm, the one who does the work may not get the bread. In this realm, it helps to have chiseled features, an inheritance, friends in high places, and higher education, but these gifts are not left under everyman's tree. Far from it. Walking beneath this sun, we rattle around in a cage of constant comparisons. As one of

Kierkegaard's pseudonyms expressed it, "The secular view always clings tightly to the difference between man and man and naturally does not have any understanding of the one thing needful . . ." (SUD, p. 33).

But that odd duck of an excogitator, the fragments of whose thoughts are strewn before us, believed that the truths about essential matters in life, about how to live, were more than less universally distributed. If this were not so, rich folks and scholars would have a better shot at salvation than the grizzled man who plows snow in the winter and runs that lawn service with his children in the summer. And if there was one thing that the very wealthy and preternaturally talented Kierkegaard was convinced of, it was this: in the realm of the spirit, all worldly differences, talents, and bank accounts will have no purchase.

Pascal famously said that if we could just learn to sit still for ten minutes and do without distractions, there would be no more wars. A similar insight seemed to percolate in the mind of our Pascal of the north. Rather than pass on knowledge, Kierkegaard hoped to direct us to the study of ourselves. He once confessed, "I want to make people aware so that they do not squander and waste their lives" (JN, vol. 4, Journal NB: 137, p. 94). And by squandering and spilling our lives he meant, among other things, half purposefully losing the understanding that we are fundamentally eternal beings, with an aspect of ourselves existing outside the flow of time. The insistence that we are more than our brains and bodies might offend Enlightenment sensibilities, but that was what Kierkegaard felt commanded to try to believe. Judging from the words that streamed from his stylus, I suspect that his efforts were not entirely in vain.

With the aim of awakening himself and others, Kierkegaard developed a theory and practice of what he termed "indirect communication." The basic tenet was that you should know where you are calling from and to whom you are speaking, and adjust your communiqué accordingly. Write merrily for the merry and abstractedly for the abstracted.

For example, Kierkegaard believed that he lived in a world of nominal Christians who had forgotten—perhaps it would be better to say, who made a point of forgetting—what it meant to be a Christian. To remind himself and others of the nature of Christianity took some indirection on Kierkegaard's part. It was not a matter of providing a theological tome. Something more subtle, more subversive was necessary. For Kierkegaard, that something extra came in the form of his pseudonymous authorship.

Kierkegaard wrote many books under his own name, but almost all of his classic works, *Either/Or*, *Fear and Trembling*, *Philosophical Fragments*, *The Sickness Unto Death*, *The Concept of Anxiety*, had a nom de plume on the title page. Scholars have endlessly debated the question of how to interpret the pen names, but in his eponymous *The Point of View of My Work as an Author*, Kierkegaard bids us to treat the pseudonyms as though they were distinct authors. After all, they refer to and even critique one another. Hewing to Kierkegaard's instructions, I would argue that the different authors are as characters in a novel. They each glimpse life from a different window, and yet many of their observations seem to come full throated from the voice behind the voices. Accordingly, more than a few of the quotes captured in this compendium derive from one of Kierkegaard's alter egos.

In virtually every one of his works Kierkegaard moans about his fellow human beings being in a rush, as though life were a matter of getting through a calculus course or something. Kierkegaard devotee Ludwig Wittgenstein once described philosophy as "the art of thinking slowly." And yet, many if not most students will press a professor to cut to the chase and get to the point about Kierkegaard or whomever! One only knows how he would have groaned about the Twitter epoch, but Kierkegaard complained of his countrymen craving books that they could peruse during their naps, of wanting to acquire the bread of life wisdom without kneading the flour. And how might he have reacted to a book of Kierkegaard quotations?

I doubt that Kierkegaard would have had a problem with the absence of context. After all, he wrote an entire book of nothing but prefaces. Kierkegaard well understood that like a Zen koan, the truth expressed in a line or three can glister as a legitimate object of reflection and appropriation. Make no mistake about it, Kierkegaard played the scribe, copying hundreds of lines from the likes of Seneca, Cicero, Plato, Luther, and of course the Bible. Sometimes he used these apothegms to help him sharpen a point, but at other times he drew on them as a source of spiritual sustenance. In the cauldron of the break with Regine and writing *Repetition*, Kierkegaard put these words into the pen of Constantine Constantius, who in turn scribbles a letter to his "Silent Confidant": " . . . Have you really read Job? Read him, read him again and again. I do not even have the heart to write one single outcry from him in a letter to you, even though I find my joy in transcribing over and over everything he has said, sometimes in Danish script and sometimes in Latin script, sometimes in one format and sometimes in another" (R, p. 204).

As I hope this text reveals, there are many sentences from Kierkegaard that, even standing alone, both open a vista onto Kierkegaard's mind and nurture the centrifugal thought he so artfully and passionately encouraged.

When it came to the pulsating question of how best to live, Kierkegaard and his pseudonyms preached that we should think of life from a first-person perspective. There are many who enjoy deliberating on theories of love, ethics, and whether or not the soul is immortal, but Kierkegaard held that these are problems the answers to which fundamentally define who you are. To contemplate them from a third-person point of view is for him a contradiction in terms. Take for, example, the issue of whether or not the soul is immortal. Kierkegaard's lyrical but philosophical persona, Johannes Climacus, writes,

> Honor be to learning! Honor be to the one who can learnedly treat the learned question of immortality! But

essentially the question of immortality is not a learned question; it is a question belonging to inwardness, which the subject by becoming himself must ask himself. (CUP, p. 173)

Climacus continues, "Objectively the question cannot be answered at all, because objectively the question of immortality cannot be asked, since immortality is precisely the intensification and highest development of the developed subjectivity" (CUP, p. 173).

Later, in the same text, the author jabs that people who have been in flux their whole lives, who have never developed inner continuity, anxiously ask whether or not they will be the same in heaven.

Unlike other philosophers, Kierkegaard did not seek to generate general theories but instead was always riveted to the individual's relationship to ideas—which for him meant grappling not with the cause or explanations but with the issue of *meaning*. Indeed, fierce attention to the question of meaning, insistence on the inside-out approach to existence, in contrast to looking for a code, theory, or a step-by-step instruction manual, is part of the reason Kierkegaard is widely regarded as the father of existentialism.

Given the enormous accent on the first person, permit me to open the door and bring myself ever so briefly into the picture. I have been walking with this strange Dane for decades. Like all relationships, ours has had its peaks and valleys. There have been times when I have shaken my head in disgust at Kierkegaard's violent judgments on others, such as when he states, "Most men are characterized by a dialectic of indifference and live a life so far from the good (faith) that it is almost too spiritless to be called sin . . ." (SUD, p. 101). Even for his era, Kierkegaard's views on women were much less than enlightened, and he has, perhaps rightfully, been accused of anti-Semitism. It is also troubling that the rich man who never had to wear the yoke of working for someone else seems less than urgent about economic inequalities and assuaging the suffering of the poor. Kierkegaard's repugnance for anything that rings of the need for reciprocity is a stone in the shoe as well. Nietzsche observed that genius is not just a matter of gray matter but of being able to tolerate mega-voltage inspiration over long intervals. Like all thinkers who burn like torches, the incandescent Kierkegaard had his dark maniacal side and blind spots. But, oh, the effulgent light and epiphanies powerful enough to help his readers see themselves from a new perspective.

I came to Kierkegaard crawling on cut glass and on the tail of a brutal marital breakup. I had dropped out of graduate school for the second time. My untethered life was like a page from a newspaper blowing around in the wind. Who knows how these things happen, but I picked up his *Works of Love* in a bookstore/coffee shop. Like a therapist, the immortal dead man helped me to understand that when the earthquakes of existence come, letting yourself sink will lead only to sinking deeper. There is no bottom. I can't cite the verse, but Kierkegaard helped me to grasp that psychological suffering was not a stench but something a person could do well or poorly. His way of recasting the landscape of human existence helped float my spirit when I was going under in ways that were positively chilling to everyone around me.

Again, "we are not in any hurry" or if you are in a hurry, you can fast-forward to Kierkegaard's own words. But then again, if you have the time, perhaps you will follow me as I reflect on a few more of the guide-wire ideas that I found in the writings of this Mozart of the spirit. Here, for instance, is a quiet diary entry that grabbed me by the collar:

> In every generation, most people . . . live and die in the delusion that things keep on going, and that if it were granted them to live longer, things would keep going onward in a continuing, straightforward ascent with more and more comprehension. How many experience at all the maturity of discovering that there comes a critical point where things turn around, when what matters from then on is an increasing comprehension that more and more comprehends that there is something that cannot be comprehended[?] (JN, vol. 6, Journal NB12: 134, p. 225)

In a sense, this entry is another inscription of the warning against that acidulating feeling of "I'm late. I'm late for a very important date," as though our eternal lives depended on amassing chestnuts of wisdom and knowledge. In the end, more knowledge is not going to bring the peace and salvation that every Nicodemus craves.

But what is involved with understanding "more and more," that there is something of fundamental importance that cannot be understood? How does the understanding understand that life is not just a matter of understanding? What does it mean for the intellect to step aside? Perhaps that we all need to muster the ability to live with cavernous uncertainty about matters of piercing importance. Given the unquenchable human desire to be in control, bowing to the unknown involves learning to abide with the anxiety lapping at our ankles and threatening to take us out to sea.

Sometimes Kierkegaard portrays anxiety as a teacher, at other times as a surgeon. In *The Concept of Anxiety*, his pseudonym Vigilius Haufniensis teaches that the individual who properly understands anxiety will sense it coming on and think, "Now I am ready. Then anxiety enters into his soul and searches out everything and anxiously torments everything finite and petty out of him . . ." (CA, p. 159).

Unlike his more rationalistic brethren, who regarded the emotions as impediments to reason, Kierkegaard believed that we have much to learn from our moods and feelings. Again, like Pascal, who wrote of reasons of the heart, Kierkegaard held that there are lessons we cannot absorb save through the heart. It is in anxiety that we come to fathom the teeth-gnashing fact that we are free to do whatever we choose. It is through that feeling, which sometimes feels like a weight, that we appropriate our freedom. For better but often worse, our anxieties can tell us where our hearts are. And to listen to Magister Kierkegaard, if we sit still for the lesson and refrain from latching on to and obsessing about some finite end, angst can help us discern the difference between finite concerns and something else.

Today anxiety is regarded as a blight. Kierkegaard is aware that the feeling we throw pills at can beat a path to transgression and guilt, then to more anxiety, and so on and so forth. But anxiety, like despair, is also the palm print of spirit. Of the individual who boasts " . . . the great thing about him is that he has never been in anxiety" (CA, p. 157), the author of *The Concept of Anxiety* responds, "I will gladly provide him with my explanation: that is because he is very spiritless" (CA, p. 157).

In the introduction to the same text and in the guise of a psychologist, Kierkegaard stressed the significance of moods. There is, he observes, a proper mood for every concept. Pondering sin, he writes, "Whenever the issue of sin is dealt with, one can observe by the very mood whether the concept is the correct one. For instance whenever sin is spoken of as a disease, an abnormality, a poison, or a disharmony, the concept is falsified" (CA, p. 25). In other terms, wrong mood, wrong concept. And thus, an academic who reflects on the Holocaust in a puzzling mood, as grist for the mill of scholarly publications, would have missed the conceptual boat.

Thought and feeling are intertwined. In a footnote, Kierkegaard/Haufniensis explains, "That science, just as much as poetry and art, presupposes a mood in the creator as well as in the observer, and that an error in the modulation is just as disturbing as an error in the development of thought, have been entirely forgotten in our time, when inwardness has been completely forgotten, and also the category of appropriation . . ." (CA, p. 14n).

Present a text to a college student and his or her first reaction will be "I like that idea" or "I don't like it" as though ideas could be tasted like different flavors of gelato. Every notion that bubbles into consciousness is attended with a feeling and the feeling that accompanies an idea reveals much about our personal relationship to that idea. According to Kierkegaard's constant complaint, no one cares at all anymore about this inner modulation.

Kierkegaard's laser focus on inwardness bends a bit in his pellucid "At a Graveside." An offering in the series *Three Discourses on Imagined Situations*, this reflection is a skull on the desk. In our own age, we like to play almost counterphobically with visions of the end. Curled up on the couch and munching popcorn, we gobble thousands of images of death on the flat screen every week. But as for the real thing, that is another story. Some of us would like to pretend that if we just eat enough kale and go to our yoga and mindfulness classes, we can keep death on the other side of the door. Like Tolstoy's *Death of Ivan Ilyich*, "At a Graveside" crafts a reminder of the retrogressive power given by the bone-deep understanding of our own mortality.

Kierkegaard wrote the masterful *Repetition*, and one aspect of his writing genius is his ability to effectively repeat himself with ever so slight changes. A veritable existential fugue, "At a Graveside" rings with no fewer than a dozen reminders that there comes a time when "all is over"—when we cannot add or alter a line to our life's story.

The Epicureans used to argue that where death is I am not—ergo, we ought never to fear our own demise. Kierkegaard chuckles at this attempt to keep death outside ourselves. In this discourse, he maintains that thinking of myself and my death together rings an alarm—and he is not here talking about waking up in time to smell the flowers—but to being less careless about the kind of persons we are becoming.

In *The Concept of Anxiety*, Kierkegaard underscores the importance of mood, but in "At a Graveside" he argues that earnestness is something over and above a mood. Like anxiety and despair, earnestness reveals that the self is a self-relating activity. We are creatures who are constituted by a special relationship to ourselves, and as such we not only are visited by thoughts and emotions, but also have the task of interpreting and relating ourselves to those thoughts and emotions. For instance, yesterday I was out for a walk. A memory drips of a deed of which I am not particularly proud. The images come with a powerful sinking feeling. I can either swoon into a despondent mood and then perhaps say or do something else that I might regret, or, in earnestness, I can pat the mood on the back, sending it along and resolving to change my ways.

The self for Kierkegaard is a kind of meta-entity. The earnest individual is able to keep a third eye on the flow of moods and recognize when they might lull him or her into forgetting what is important in life. For all of his screeds about the dangers of reflection, it is to this internal relating activity that Kierkegaard, from different corners of his study and in diverse voices, addresses himself.

Kierkegaard was a fundamentalist about "the self" and "the individual." Does this mark him as a precursor to our own culture of narcissism? No less than Kierkegaard, the present age is also obsessed with the care of the self. Self-esteem fanatics, we postmodern men and women are haunted by worries of the sort that we are just not getting enough out of life, not realizing our full potentials. The burning question is "Can we have it all?" but the fretting is often about checks on a bucket list of experiences and accomplishments.

Most of us feel more urgency about the size of our waistline than about the girth of our capacity for compassion. Doing the right thing still has valence, but it is just one option among many, as in, I want to be a successful lawyer, have a good marriage and family, and be a good guy. Often by daubing a picture that the reader can see himself or herself in, Kierkegaard tries to kindle a concern about the self, but with a different set of categories up his sleeves than we are likely to find in the likes of *Eat, Pray, Love* and the boundless literature of the self-help and happiness market.

Aristotle taught that there is a degree of precision appropriate to every subject matter. In other terms, you ought not to expect the same measure of clarity in discussing ethics that you would in physics. Kierkegaard was alive to this point. In his *Works of Love*, he baldly stated, "All human speech, even divine speech of Holy Scripture, about the spiritual is essentially metaphorical speech" (WL, p. 209); in other words, messy and imprecise. When we talk about external objects, we can examine them together to make sure that we are referring to the same thing—not so when we discuss the spirit or the self.

This admission is of paramount importance given the fact that almost every word that dripped from Kierkegaard's pen had something to do with the life of the spirit. In his *Philosophy and the Mirror of Nature*, Richard Rorty wisely observed that philosophers tend to spin webs of metaphors only to quickly forget that they are speaking figuratively. It is easy to forget that the spatial images that Kierkegaard hones to describe our inner lives are, by his own accounting, only a rough description of the spiritual realm. From the first page to the last, our Galileo of the inner world described the vicissitudes of the spirit in terms of movement. There is the movement of infinite resignation daubed in *Fear and Trembling*, and in the same work the "movement of faith" is described in self-consciously paradoxical terms of giving up the world and getting it back, or of the detaching from the world and yet being fully present in it.

A central chord of Kierkegaard's thinking on earnestness and faith resonates with Buddhist notions about enlightenment. Kierkegaard frequently frames the image of dying to the world to provide a glimpse of what is involved in coming alive spiritually. Among other things, this means not directing infinite passion to finite ends, not having your sense of self consumed with worries about whether or not you pass the bar exam or marry Jack or Jill. For all the angst that comes with our heart's worldly desires, in a backhanded way they provide something tangible to grab onto in life. If I just land this job I will be whole, or if only so and so loved me, I could don a "Life is Good" T-shirt. In America we are virtually indoctrinated with the notion that we should chase after some dream about ourselves, something that the psychoanalyst Alfred Adler called a "fictional finalism."

For Kierkegaard these ego visions, at least when they rise to a certain pitch, are a form of despair. In the crown jewel of his authorship, *The Sickness Unto Death*, a pseudonym very close to Kierkegaard's heart, Anti-Climacus, observes,

An individual in despair despairs over *something*. So it seems for a moment, but only for a moment; in the same moment the true despair or despair in its true form shows itself. In despairing over *something*, he really despaired over *himself*, and now he wants to get rid of himself. For example, when the ambitious man whose slogan is "Either Caesar or nothing" does not get to be Caesar, he despairs over it. But this also means something else: precisely because he did not get to be Caesar, he now cannot bear to be himself. Consequently he does not despair because he did not get to be Caesar but despairs over himself because he did not get to be Caesar. This self, which, if it had become Caesar, would have been in seventh heaven (a state, incidentally, that in another sense is just as despairing), this self is now utterly intolerable to him. (SUD, p. 19)

Despair represents a misrelation in the self. In most cases, it could also be described as a willed and semi-conscious ignorance of what it means to be a self. Those individuals who live by the shibboleth "Caesar or nothing"—get into med school or the *New Yorker* or nothing—cannot bear being themselves without these badges. They have placed the axis of themselves outside of themselves. This is one of the great perils of the fundamentalism about dreams in the United States. But as is often the case with Kierkegaard, the most important lines are threaded into the parenthesis.

If the man had realized his ambition and become Caesar, he would have been in a state "that in another sense is just as despairing." He would have been in seventh heaven and in despair. This would of course be an unconscious form of despair. For Kierkegaard, almost everything having to do with our inner lives is dialectical. It can mean one thing or the other. A sense of peace and contentment can indicate that you have been cured of despair, but more often than not it shrouds a misrelation in the self. People who are in the pink—who, as the saying goes, "have it all," family, career, friendship, stability, adventure, good looks, and good conscience too, are least likely to grasp that they are barreling down the wrong road, in the opposite direction from becoming the individuals that they were meant to be.

The notion of the unconscious was beginning to seep into consciousness in Kierkegaard's time. Like that other astronomer of the universe behind the brows, Sigmund Freud, Kierkegaard understood that what comes into awareness is only one set of rooms in our psychic lives. Perhaps the most potent use that Kierkegaard puts the concept of the unconscious to is in uncovering the corrosive powers of self-deception and the impact of the self-hoodwinking process on our moral lives.

In *The Sickness Unto Death*, Kierkegaard's Anti-Climacus is trying to fathom what health and sickness ultimately mean. In Part I of this volume, despair is defined as an imbalance in the self and, a few pages later, in terms of gradations of consciousness of being a self. At the one end, there are those who are oblivious to the notion that they might be something more than a network of experiences; at the other extreme, there is the defiant form of despair in which the individual has a sense of the calling card of the eternal but refuses to pick it up because he or she insists on being a self on his or her own terms. In the second portion of the book the author unequivocally announces, "Despair is sin." But then what is sin? Here, Anti-Climacus turns to his pagan patron saint Socrates, and investigates the possibility that sin is ignorance. At first, the doctor of the soul seems to reject the Socratic conception of sin. After all, we cannot be held culpable for doing something wrong when we were ignorant of the fact that it is wrong to begin with—unless, of course, we are guilty of producing the ignorance that led to the wrongdoing.

In this section, Kierkegaard's favorite pseudonym is puzzling over the fact that we humans are capable of passionately preaching one line and then doing the exact opposite. He exclaims,

> [I]t is tragic-comic to see that all this knowledge and understanding exercises no power at all over men's lives, that their lives do not express in the remotest way what they have understood, but rather the opposite.... It is exceedingly comic that a man, stirred to tears so that not only sweat but also tears pour down his face, can sit and read or hear an exposition on self-denial, on the nobility of sacrificing his life for the truth—and then in the next moment, *ein, zwei, drei, vupti,* almost with tears still in his eyes, be in full swing, in the sweat of his brow and to the best of his modest ability, helping untruth to be victorious. (SUD, p. 90–91)

A few pages later there is something approaching an explanation:

> In the life of the spirit there is no standing still ... if a person does not do what is right at the very second he knows it—then, first of all, knowing simmers down. Next comes the question of how willing appraises what is known. (SUD, p. 94)

Here we have the tripartite model of the self that we find in Plato, Aristotle, and Freud. The understanding and the will are about to enter into a dialogue, but

Willing is dialectical and has under it the entire lower nature of man. If willing does not agree with what is known, then it does not necessarily follow that willing goes ahead and does the opposite of what knowing understood (presumably such strong opposites are rare); rather, willing allows some time to elapse, an interim called: "We shall look at it tomorrow." During all this, knowing becomes more and more obscure, and the lower nature gains the upper hand more and more; alas, for the good must be done immediately, as soon as it is known . . . (SUD, p. 94)

And now the warning:

[B]ut the lower nature's power lies in stretching things out. Gradually, willing's objection to this development lessens; it almost appears to be in collusion. And when knowing has become duly obscured, knowing and willing can better understand each other; eventually they agree completely, for now knowing has come over to the side of willing and admits that what it wants is absolutely right. (SUD, p. 94)

At this juncture, Kierkegaard's psychoanalysis competes with Freud's. To listen to Kierkegaard, it is as though a constant whispering conversation were taking place between our lower nature, our selfish desires, and the will. Like Augustine, Kierkegaard and his pseudonyms portray daily life as though we were in a constant battle with time. Procrastination is not a vice to joke about. In time, we can convince ourselves of almost anything. Given a few days or maybe just a few hours, we can talk ourselves into believing that the easy path is the right path, that we are morally obligated to do just what we want to do. It was because of our magic powers of self-deception that Kierkegaard judged hypocrisy to be a rarity. We don't preach one thing and do another; instead we change by increments what we are preaching to accommodate our desires.

The decision is suddenly in your lap—do you sacrifice a portion of your vacation days to pitch in with a community project to help the homeless? After all, you were a passionate advocate of the project, recruiting friends, and so on. Unfortunately, you didn't realize that an essential part of the effort would fall during your vacation. What do you do? Nothing rash, says good sense. Perhaps you should give yourself a little time to think about it, and as you mull over the matter you slowly come to realize that you can't take care of anyone else unless you take care of yourself. The next thing you know, the right thing to do is to throw down a towel and relax in the sun. And so it goes. Knowledge comes over to the side of desire, but according to Kierkegaard, it is always with some subliminal awareness that the righteous path leads to a car crash with our long- and short-term prospects for happiness. Anti-Climacus drives to this inconvenient conclusion: "And this is how perhaps the great majority of men live: they work gradually at eclipsing their ethical and ethical-religious comprehension, which would lead them out into decisions and conclusions that their lower nature does not much care for but they expand their esthetic and metaphysical comprehension . . ." (SUD, p. 94).

We increase our store of knowledge about the world, but our moral and spiritual understanding becomes diminished. As time ticks by, we expect less and less from ourselves, morally speaking. It is, no doubt, for this reason that we tend to think of youth as a period of enchanted idealism, a time from which we awaken and come to our senses, or as Kierkegaard would have it, slip into a moral and spiritual slumber.

As for sin, the text continues, " . . . sin is not a matter of a person's not having understood what is right but of his being unwilling to understand it, of his not willing what is right" (SUD, p. 95). Or put another way, "Therefore, interpreted Christianly, sin has its roots in willing, not in knowing, and this corruption of willing embraces the individual's consciousness" (SUD, p. 95).

Many scholars have taken up the project of trying to articulate something like a Kierkegaardian ethic. However, Kierkegaard thought much more in terms of the sin/faith dichotomy than good and evil. Still, if Kierkegaard is correct, then one of the moral assignments in life is to look into our own eyes and be honest with ourselves. It is not more ethics classes and experts that we need. Ethically speaking, it is not knowledge that we lack, but the resolve to hold on to what we know by abjuring from rationalizations. At bottom, even this admonition is rooted in a religious sensibility, for like Dostoyevsky, Kierkegaard believed that you cannot become transparent to yourself, cannot properly read your inner life outside the light of the God relation.

Kierkegaard's depth psychology and his views on self-deception also find expression in his *Works of Love*. In that text, love is presented as a salmagundi of seemingly immiscible qualities, a passion, a need, a feeling, and above all a duty. Although Kierkegaard describes a defense of faith as something akin to heresy, he occasionally pokes with the suggestion that the central ideas of Christianity, for example, that we have a duty to love, are so alien that no human could have ever come up with the idea.

The first page of *Works of Love* is a sheet of pure light. Just read:

> If it were so, as conceited sagacity, proud of not being deceived, thinks, that we should believe nothing that we cannot see with our physical eyes, then we first and foremost ought to give up believing in love. If we were to do so out of fear lest we be deceived, would we not then be deceived? We can, of course, be deceived in many ways. We can be deceived by believing what is untrue, but we certainly are also deceived by not believing what is true. (WL, p. 5)

Love is a risk. Again and again, Kierkegaard hammers; there is a risk to being shrewd, calculating, and risk-averse. On the next page, the connection between love and self-deception is developed:

> Ordinarily, when it is a matter of being deceived [*bedrages*] in love, however different the case may be, the one deceived is still related to love, and the deception is

only that the love was not where it was thought to be, but the self-deceived person has locked and is locking himself out of love. (WL, p. 6)

This insight about locking ourselves out of love applies at two levels; it speaks to our relationships with others but primarily for Kierkegaard with locking ourselves out of our God relationship.

I have heard this sort of remark before, sometimes from my own lips: "Religion and all this talk of God is a basically a bunch of ghost stories. I'm not going to waste this, my only life, and perhaps what is most precious to me in this life on some imperceptible father figure that is supposed to exist, who knows where." For fear of being deceived and not getting the most out of life, every Doubting Thomas is hoodwinked, for again, you can be deceived by refusing to believe what is true just as easily as you can by being taken in by what is false.

Kierkegaard's instruction on learning to love will prompt the therapists to shake their heads. He writes, "The matter is quite simple. A person should begin with loving the unseen, God, because then he himself will learn what it is to love. But that he actually loves the unseen will be known by his loving the brother he sees; the more he loves the unseen, the more he will love the people he sees" (WL, p. 160).

The man who knew *amore* but never happy love warns that a love that is not commanded is always a preferential love, that is, a strand of love in which you adore a person for her gimlet eyes, or maybe her ability to listen but always because she has some quality that is of value to you. Kierkegaard insists that this kind of love, and the "fastidious" quality-attentive mind-set that goes along with it is, at bottom, a form of self-love.

Because love is all-inclusive, Kierkegaard allows that marriage and falling for the person of your checklist dreams can be included under the umbrella of his austere conception, but nonetheless, on his reading of the New Testament, we must first and foremost relate to lovers and friends as neighbors whom we are commanded to love. Then, he thinks, love becomes ennobled into something more than tingling and titivated, fundamentally selfish desire.

In his *Civilization and Its Discontents*, Freud quietly rages at this Christian notion of universal and uncontingent love, arguing that it is nothing less than a sin against love. For Freud, love is our most cherished gift, the giving of which renders us an open wound. To him, the idea of loving indiscriminately was pure pathology. In a sense, Kierkegaard concedes Freud's point; from a secular vantage point the claim that the only true love is one that does not acknowledge differences is an abomination. And yet, Kierkegaard would counter that it was not familial love or romantic love that Christ was describing when he made love a duty and commanded "love your neighbors as yourself." But at the risk of seeming a pedant or Pharisee, there is another puzzle here—how do we, and how are we supposed to, love ourselves?

Anyone with a modicum of psychological sensibilities knows very well that true self-love is hard to find.

Glimpsed from the window of that study in Copenhagen, truly loving oneself is akin to worrying about the kind of person you are becoming. The concern that Kierkegaard finds constitutive of the self is not a matter of worrying about landing a job with benefits and paying back your student loans, but maybe something closer to questions, such as, can you put yourself aside and maybe skip that eighty-mile bike ride you were looking forward to and help that kid down the block prepare for his GED?

As already noted, Kierkegaard was a severe critic of the fantasy that we can and should endeavor to think about life and the hurly-burly of our existence from some kind of universal, perspectiveless perspective. He saw the present age as one in which people strove for impartiality and the kind of objectivity you might expect from a jury member or scientist. As he understood it, the secular edict was to suppress an interest in oneself, which for Kierkegaard was a form of spiritual suicide (cf. TA, p. 68). It is a suicide because it tends to amplify worries about careers while it mutes and sneers at the notion of fretting about becoming a self in the deeper Kierkegaardian sense.

But then again, we live in a fragmented world of buzzing screens and surfaces; maybe all these references to "something deeper" are a ruse. Whether it be Plato's eternal forms or the Christian mansion beyond the sky, Nietzsche retched over the constant appeal to "a world behind the scenes"—a world that was always held to be more real than the warmth of the sun and shimmering sea. The philosopher with the hammer and tong warned that there was also arsenic in the appeals to a real self "deep inside," and so on. Georges Brandes, the Danish critic, passed Kierkegaard's works on to Nietzsche, but it was at a time when Nietzsche was deep into the madness he would ride for the last decade of his life. But even if it had been in his healthiest days, Nietzsche would have found Kierkegaard to be the most sublime and dangerous poison, a poison that makes us second-guess our strongest pulse beats.

Kierkegaard, however, was possessed of an ardent faith that what made us human was the willingness to trust in and bend our lives to the contours of something unseen and beyond reason. As Orwell wrote of Gandhi, much the same can be said for Kierkegaard: His "teachings cannot be squared with the belief that Man is the measure of all things and that our job is to make life worth living on this earth, which is the only earth we have. They make sense only on the assumption that God exists. . . ."* One can only wonder how Kierkegaard might have replied to someone who earnestly pressed, why should I devote my life to a God whom I can't see and who, if he is there, has not taken the best of care of me? The thinker, who in life could not dance, but who was the subtlest and most supple of intellectual ballet artists, once suggested that the best answer to that question of why believe might be "Because your father told you." It's his famous Either/Or. Choose.

* George Orwell, "Reflections on Gandhi" (1949).

A Note on Quote Selection

Permit me a confession and a few words on the selection of quotes in this text. Robert Hamilton has been quoted as saying, "a book of quotations . . . can never be complete." That is especially true with a volume of Kierkegaard's quotations. A word-gem collector could easily fill four volumes of epiphanic sentences from this thinker. In my selection, I have worked from that corner of the corpus where I have spent the bulk of my many years with Kierkegaard, that is, on those studies that bear on the psychology of our moral and religious lives. Of course, Kierkegaard often has the feather touch in delivering his weighty wisdom, but caveat emptor, this book is not "The Lighter Side of Kierkegaard." As the wise and often hilarious *The Humor of Kierkegaard* (Princeton University Press) attests, there is a lighter and wittier side of Kierkegaard than the one encased in these covers. And that side of the man is not to be disparaged. For Kierkegaard, the face of earnestness/seriousness, a quality that he circles around on every page, is not a scowl. There is a reason the Buddha often looks as though he were about to break into a chuckle. Just listen to the jest in which Kierkegaard tenderly and half kidding, tethers the gods (religion), laughter, and life.

> Something marvelous has happened to me. I was transported to the seventh heaven. There sat all the gods assembled. As a special dispensation, I was granted the favor of making a wish. "What do you want," asked Mer-

cury. . . . "Choose—but only one thing." For a moment I was bewildered; then I addressed the gods, saying: My esteemed contemporaries, I choose one thing—that I may always have the laughter on my side. Not one of the gods said a word; instead, all of them began to laugh. From that I concluded that my wish was granted and decided that the gods knew how to express themselves with good taste, for it would indeed have been inappropriate to reply solemnly: It is granted to you. (EO,1, pp. 42–43)

The line with our author addressing the gods as "my esteemed contemporaries" is just delicious. It almost goes without saying that irony, humor, wit, belly laughter, and jest are serious matters for Kierkegaard. Just the same, Kierkegaard was not jesting when he repeatedly insisted that we turn into, not away from, the self-concern that is for him the ethereal embodiment of earnestness. As I confessed in the introduction, I came to Kierkegaard desperately seeking life guidance. Many of the branches that I have clipped from the tree of wisdom that is Kierkegaard's writings are measured not for their cleverness, but against Kierkegaard's criterion, "Only the truth that edifies is the truth for Thee."

KIERKEGAARD'S BIOGRAPHY

Despite the fact that he seldom took written note of it, Kierkegaard was always on the *qui vive* for what he termed "hints" from God. For instance, at one point late in life, Kierkegaard bumps into the father of his former fiancée, and he puts off publishing a book, as he waits to see if the encounter is a divine message. I wonder how those who are open to the idea of such hints from on high might interpret the fact that the thinker who was consumed with the question of what it means to have faith was named "Kierkegaard"—which translated into English means churchyard.

The intellectual and spiritual comet that was Søren Aabye Kierkegaard began his days on earth on May 5, 1813. Born in Copenhagen, he was the youngest of seven children born to Michael Pedersen Kierkegaard and his second wife and former servant, Anne Sørensdatter Lund. Michael Pedersen's first wife died childless two years after their marriage, and he married his wife's maid. In something of a public embarrassment, they had their first child five months after their wedding. The ages of Kierkegaard's parents were almost biblical for the time. His mother was forty-five when Søren was born and his father fifty-six.

A native of Jutland, Michael Pedersen Kierkegaard (1756–1838) began life as a poor shepherd boy on the heaths of Jutland. One unholy day he was so distraught about his hardscrabble lot that he cursed God. His lot soon changed. At twelve, an uncle took him in to work in his dry-goods business in Copenhagen. In time, he went out on his own and became a highly successful textile merchant. He also invested in real estate and stocks and was soon so well off that his progeny would never have to fret about making a living.

The Kierkegaard family was among the nouveaux riches of the Danish capitol city. They were also members of a pietistic community with strong ties to the Moravians.

In the many volumes of personal jottings, Kierkegaard does not devote a single word to his mother, and yet his journals reverberate with reflections about his father. Kierkegaard's stern, melancholic, pious, and indisputably brilliant autodidact of an old man left an unusually deep impress on him. Some would call it a scar.

Before Søren was twenty-one, four of his siblings, a number of in-laws, and his mother had been buried. At one point, Michael Pedersen confided that the endless treks to the cemetery were all part of a divine punishment for his boyhood curse against God. The elder Kierkegaard announced to his remaining sons, Peter and Søren, that he would outlive all his children, that he was damned "to be a cross upon their graves." Søren believed him.

As for Kierkegaard's formative years, the immortal genius was a very good but not a stellar student at the Copenhagen School of Civic Virtue. Years after Kierkegaard's death, Frederik Welding, a fellow classmate, recalled,

> He was always number two or three in the various classes in which we were students. He was a skinny boy, always on the run, and he could never keep from giving free rein to his whimsy and from teasing others with nicknames he had heard, with laughter, and with funny faces, even though it often earned him a beating. I do not recall that his language was ever genuinely witty or cutting, but it was annoying and provocative, and he was aware that it had this effect even though he was often the one who paid for it. (Kirmmse, *Encounters with Kierkegaard*, p. 7)

As though a harbinger of things to come, the young Kierkegaard was called *gaflen* or "the fork" in part for his ability to discern the vulnerabilities of others and his delight in sticking it to them. And of course, he would one day stick his tines into both the bourgeois mentality and Christendom.

Kierkegaard matriculated in theology at the University of Copenhagen in 1830, taking classes in a wide range of subjects including philosophy, mathematics, physics, Greek, Hebrew, and Latin, in which he excelled. He took his sweet time at the university and to some extent lived the life of a flaneur, spending hours and much money as he mingled in café society. His father reprimanded him for the enormous bills that he was running up and his wayward lifestyle as well as for the slow pace of his university studies.

The pater familias died in 1838. Kierkegaard was shocked to have outlived his father. Maintaining that he could not argue with a dead man, the prodigal was supercharged with energy and completed his studies in a veritable flash. In July 1840 he passed his exams at the university and in 1841 he publicly defended his magister (doctoral) dissertation, *The Concept of Irony with Constant Reference to Socrates*. Kierkegaard was such a polemical figure that one of the members of his dissertation committee may have feigned illness rather than exchange intellectual jabs and counters with Kierkegaard at his doctoral defense.

But there was another event that marked the man who would leave such a mark on the world of ideas. In 1837, when he was twenty-four and a university student, Kierkegaard became enamored of the fifteen-year-old Regine Olsen. A little over three years later they became engaged. Immediately, Kierkegaard began to have second and third thoughts, and after thirteen months he terminated the engagement. Regine was distraught. Fearful for his daughter's health and even life, Regine's father, Councilor Olsen, humbly begged Kierkegaard to reconsider—but Kierkegaard would not relent. In his *nachlass*, he would sometimes suggest that he broke off their engagement to protect Regine from the profound melancholy that afflicted his family; on other pages, he intimated that he could not dance with the ideas that were burbling behind his eyes and be home for dinner at five.

In a couple years' time, Regine recovered from the emotional trauma and married Johan Frederik Schlegel, who later became governor of the Danish West Indies. Still, perhaps in a highly poeticized fashion, Regine remained the queen of Kierkegaard's heart. Though it would be enough to make any therapist wince, Kierkegaard believed that if you truly loved someone, it was for keeps. There was no getting over it and "moving on." A true lover "keeps this love young, and it grows along with him in years and in beauty" (FT, p. 44). For as the author of *Fear and Trembling* tells it, "he is too proud to be willing to let the whole substance of his life turn out to have been an affair of the fleeting moment" (FT, p. 44).

In 1841, two weeks after ending his engagement, and in part to help make the break easier for Regine, Kierkegaard departed for Berlin. There he attended the lectures of the renowned German philosopher Friedrich Schelling. It was in the vibrant German city and the crucible of the split with Regine that Kierkegaard came into his Muse. In four months and while attending classes at the University of Berlin, he penned the immense and immortal *Either/Or* as well as *Two Upbuilding Discourses*. In March 1841, having had his fill of Schelling, Kierkegaard returned to Copenhagen, where he continued his prodigious literary productivity. Over the next three years, Kierkegaard held the

wire of a kind of intellectual stimulation that few people ever feel and fewer still can tolerate for any length
of time. During that period, he composed *Fear and
Trembling*, *Repetition*, *The Concept of Anxiety*, *Philosophical Fragments*, *Stages on Life's Way*, and a shelf of
"upbuilding discourses." All the while, he was scribbling like a fiend in his journals.

In 1844, Kierkegaard resolved that after one more
book he would lay down his pen and, though almost
comic to consider, take a post as a country pastor! His
literary finale was to be *The Concluding Unscientific
Postscript*—"concluding" because it was to be his final
book, "unscientific" so as to distinguish it from the sys-
tematizing work of Hegel, and "postscript" relative to
the *Philosophical Fragments*. But then fate or something higher intervened.

In December 1845, P. L. Møller put out a critical
review of Kierkegaard's pseudonymously published
Stages on Life's Way. Møller often published anony-
mously in *The Corsair*, a popular magazine special-
izing in political satire. For all his gray matter and
confidence, Kierkegaard was a highly umbrageous
individual. In January of that year, Kierkegaard, writing under the guise of Frater Taciturnus (one of
the pseudonymous authors of *Stages on Life's Way*),
launched an attack on Møller and *The Corsair*. This
was a time of great political turmoil in Denmark as
well as the rest of Europe. Indeed, in 1848 Denmark
would make the peaceful transition to a constitu-
tional monarchy. By connecting Møller with the
widely circulating left-wing periodical, Kierkegaard

delivered a crippling and, most believe, low blow to Møller's academic aspirations.

The Corsair responded to Kierkegaard's attack with a torrent of articles and brilliant caricatures, always picturing Kierkegaard as vain and narcissistic. In one illustration, our author is artfully depicted riding on Regine's back with a whip in hand. There is another of him in formal dress and top hat, arms folded and musing as the world appears to revolve around him. Kierkegaard soon became a negative media star—or, as he described it, "a martyr of laughter." The man who delighted in ambling around the streets of Copenhagen and talking with everyone from fishmongers to government ministers could no longer make his rounds without attracting a crowd. In his turn, Kierkegaard returned fire with his pen. By the end of the following year, Meir Goldschmidt, editor of *The Corsair*, resigned. Kierkegaard had won the battle but lost the war; his private life was never the same again. No doubt, this bloody episode, which "The Fork" was certainly guilty of escalating, helped form his very low but perhaps percipient views about the press and the steamrolling abstraction he called "The Public."

After the *Corsair* affair, Kierkegaard retired any ideas he had of retiring from his scribbling life. In 1849, he published the Christian psychological masterpiece *The Sickness Unto Death*. I believe this study represents Kierkegaard at the summit of his powers.

In 1851, Kierkegaard began a period that is widely regarded as the black hole in his life. Though he continued keeping his diary, his publications, which up to this point had flowed like a mighty river, now only dribbled. Again, largely on account of the *Corsair* incident, Kierkegaard could no longer take his "people baths" in the streets. He led an increasingly isolated and lonely existence. In addition, he was running out of his inheritance and was without prospects for a job, so his journal reflections sway back and forth between worrying about his financial situation and being at what he termed "the innermost center of Christianity." And then the third climactic event in Kierkegaard's otherwise writerly life occurred.

In 1854, Bishop Jacob Mynster, who had long ministered to Kierkegaard's family, died. Kierkegaard's father was devoted to Mynster, and Kierkegaard himself delivered gift copies of his books to Mynster and was always deeply concerned about where he stood with the prelate. But there was also a powerful current of ambivalence.

At Mynster's funeral, Kierkegaard's former professor, Hans Martensen, described Mynster as "a witness to the truth," one "of the whole series of witnesses to the truth which extends through time like a chain, from the days of the Apostles to our own day." Kierkegaard, who for years had been obliquely arguing that following Christ required the imitation of Christ in suffering and self-denial, was aghast at the idea that a man who enjoyed power, prestige, and luxury should be likened to those who in bearing witness were spat upon, thrashed, and ultimately executed. As early as *Fear and Trembling*, Kierkegaard was writing, "Not only in the business world but also in the world of ideas, our age stages *em wirklicher Ausverkauf* [a real sale]. Everything can be had at such a bargain price that it becomes a question whether there is finally anyone who will make a bid" (FT, p. 5). On Kierkegaard's reckoning, the deep discount was on the requirements of faith.

Kierkegaard judged Martensen's hyperbole to be a logical extension of the cheapening of religion that had long been under way. He pulled the lanyard and in a series of self-published articles blasted away at the Danish state church, demanding that Martensen explain in what sense Mynster had been a witness. To many, this was all very unseemly, for Kierkegaard was in effect critiquing the praise layered upon a revered individual in, of all things, a eulogy. Martensen offered a tepid response and then attempted to stonewall Kierkegaard; he should have known that this strategy would never work with his firebrand of a former student. Kierkegaard pounded away, detailing the ways in which the institution of Christianity was beating a path away from lives of Christian conviction and authenticity. For the first time, he stopped attending services and encouraged others to do the same—explaining that by staying home people would have one less sin to repent for, since they would no longer be participating in a process that "made a fool of God."

In the fall of 1855, Kierkegaard delivered his last fusillade. A week later, after having spent what little remained of his inheritance, he collapsed on the street. He was taken to Frederik's Hospital with his lower body in a state of paralysis. In the hospital, he refused to take communion and speak to any members of the clergy, including his brother, Peter. However, the gravely ill man did make an exception for one minister—his dear friend Emil Boesen. To him, Kierkegaard explained, "When hunters go after the wild boar they choose a certain dog and know very well what will happen: the wild boar will be trapped, but the dog who gets him will pay for it. I will gladly die. Then I will be certain that I accomplished the task. Often people would rather hear what a dead person has to say than someone who is alive" (Kirmmse, *Encounters with Kierkegaard*, p. 125).

On November 11, at the age of forty-two, the hound of heaven died from what may have been tuberculosis. In perfect harmony with the rest of his life, there was a public disturbance at the burial service in Assistens Cemetery. As Kierkegaard's estranged brother/priest, Peter, began his eulogy, Kierkegaard's nephew, Henrik Lund, stepped forward and protested the fact that his uncle, who had categorically rejected the state church, was now being buried by the church! Many in the very large crowd shouted "bravo" to Lund's words, even though the young man was told that he was not allowed to speak.

Although she refused the bequest, Kierkegaard directed that Regine Olsen receive what remained of his material possessions. He also chose these words from Hans Adolf Brorson for his headstone:

In yet a little while
I shall have won;

Then the whole fight
Will all at once be done.
Then I may rest
In bowers of roses
And perpetually
And perpetually
Speak with my Jesus.

SOURCES AND ABBREVIATIONS

BA *The Book on Adler*, edited and translated by Howard V. Hong and Edna H. Hong. Princeton University Press, 1998.

CA *The Concept of Anxiety: A Simple Psychologically Orienting Deliberation on the Dogmatic Issue of Hereditary Sin*, edited and translated by Reidar Thomte in collaboration with Albert B. Anderson. Princeton University Press, 1980.

CD *Christian Discourses: The Crisis and a Crisis in the Life of an Actress*, edited and translated by Howard V. Hong and Edna H. Hong. Princeton University Press, 1997.

CI *The Concept of Irony: With Continual Reference to Socrates*, edited and translated by Howard V. Hong and Edna H. Hong. Princeton University Press, 1992.

COR *The Corsair Affair*, by Søren Kierkegaard, edited and translated by Howard V. Hong and Edna H. Hong. Princeton University Press, 1982.

CUP *Concluding Unscientific Postscript to Philosophical Fragments*, edited and translated by Howard V.

Hong and Edna H. Hong. Vols. 1–2. Princeton University Press, 1982.

EO,1   *Either/Or Part I*, edited and translated by Howard V. Hong and Edna H. Hong. Princeton University Press, 1987.

EO,2   *Either/Or Part II*, edited and translated by Howard V. Hong and Edna H. Hong. Princeton University Press, 1990.

EUD   *Eighteen Upbuilding Discourses*, edited and translated by Howard V. Hong and Edna H. Hong. Princeton University Press, 1990.

FSE   *For Self-Examination/Judge for Yourself*, edited and translated by Howard V. Hong and Edna H. Hong. Princeton University Press, 1990.

FT/R   *Fear and Trembling/Repetition*, edited and translated by Howard V. Hong and Edna H. Hong. Princeton University Press, 1983.

JN   *Kierkegaard's Journals and Notebooks*, Bruce H. Kirmmse, General Editor. Vols. 1–6. Princeton University Press, 2007–12.

JP   *Søren Kierkegaard's Journals and Papers*, edited and translated by Howard V. Hong and Edna H. Hong. Vols. 1–7. Indiana University Press, 1967–78.

LD   *Kierkegaard Letters and Documents*, translated by Henrik Rosenmeier. Princeton University Press, 1978.

P   *Prefaces/Writing Sampler*, edited and translated by Todd W. Nichol. Princeton University Press, 1997.

PC   *Practice in Christianity*, edited and translated by Howard V. Hong and Edna H. Hong. Princeton University Press, 1991.

PF/JC *Philosophical Fragments/Johannes Climacus*, edited and translated by Howard V. Hong and Edna H. Hong. Princeton University Press, 1985.

PV *The Point of View*, edited and translated by Howard V. Hong and Edna H. Hong. Princeton University Press, 1998.

SLW *Stages on Life's Way*, edited and translated by Howard V. Hong and Edna H. Hong. Princeton University Press, 1988.

SUD *The Sickness Unto Death: A Christian Psychological Exposition for Upbuilding and Awakening*, edited and translated by Howard V. Hong and Edna H. Hong. Princeton University Press, 1983.

TA *Two Ages: The Age of Revolution and the Present Age*, edited and translated by Howard V. Hong and Edna H. Hong. Princeton University Press, 1978.

TDIO *Three Discourses on Imagined Occasions*, edited and translated by Howard V. Hong and Edna H. Hong. Princeton University Press, 1990.

TM *The Moment and Late Writings*, edited and translated by Howard V. Hong and Edna H. Hong. Princeton University Press, 1990.

UDVS *Upbuilding Discourses in Various Spirits*, edited and translated by Howard V. Hong and Edna H. Hong. Princeton University Press, 1993.

WA *Without Authority*, edited and translated by Howard V. Hong and Edna H. Hong. Princeton University Press, 1997.

WL *Works of Love*, edited and translated by Howard V. Hong and Edna H. Hong. Princeton University Press, 1995.

CHRONOLOGY

1813

May 5   Søren Aabye Kierkegaard born at Nytorv 2 (new number, 27), Copenhagen, son of Michael Pedersen Kierkegaard and Anne Sørensdatter Lund Kierkegaard.

June 3   Baptized in Helliggeist Church in Copenhagen.

1821

Enrolls in Borgerdydskolen in Copenhagen.

1828

April 20   Confirmed in Vor Frue Church by Pastor J. P. Mynster (later to become bishop).

1830

October 30   Registers as student at University of Copenhagen.

November 1   Drafted into Royal Guard, Company 7.

November 4   Discharged as unfit for service.

1831

April 25   Finishes first part of second examination (Latin, Greek, Hebrew, and history, magna cum laude; mathematics, summa cum laude).

October 27   Completes second part of second examination (philosophy, physics, and mathematics, summa cum laude).

1834

April 15   Entry 1 A 1 of journals and papers.

1837

Between May 8   On a visit to the Rørdams in Frederiksberg meets Regine Olsen for the first
and May 12   time.

Autumn   Begins teaching Latin for a term in Borgerdydskolen.

1838

August 9   Father dies.

September 7   Publication of *From the Papers of One Still Living*, by S. Kierkegaard. (About H. C. Andersen as a novelist, with special reference to his latest work, *Only a Fiddler.*)

1840

July 3   Completes examination for degree (magna cam laude).

July 19–August 6 Journey to ancestral home in Jutland.

.

| September 10 | Becomes engaged to Regine Olsen. |
| November 17 | Enters the Pastoral Seminary. |

1841

January 12	Preaches sermon in Holmens Kirke.
July 16	Dissertation for the master of arts degree, *The Concept of Irony, with Constant Reference to Socrates*, accepted.
September 29	Defends his dissertation. [Around mid-century magister degrees came to be regarded and named officially as doctoral degrees, such as they are now.]
October 11	Engagement with Regine Olsen broken.
October 25	Leaves Copenhagen for Berlin, where he attends Schelling's lectures.

1842

| March 6 | Returns to Copenhagen. |

1843

February 20	*Either/Or*, edited by Victor Eremita, published.
May 8	Leaves for short visit to Berlin.
May 16	*Two Edifying Discourses*, by S. Kierkegaard, published.
October 16	*Repetition,* by Constantine Constantius; *Fear and Trembling*, by Johannes de Silentio; and *Three Edifying Discourses*, by S. Kierkegaard, published.
December 6	*Four Edifying Discourses*, by S. Kierkegaard, published.

1844

February 24	Preaches terminal sermon in Trinitatis Church.
March 5	*Two Edifying Discourses*, by S. Kierkegaard, published.
June 8	*Three Edifying Discourses*, by S. Kierkegaard, published.
June 13	*Philosophical Fragments*, by Johannes Climacus, published.
June 17	*The Concept of Dread*, by Vigilius Haufniensis; and *Prefaces*, by Nicholaus Notabene, published.
August 31	*Four Edifying Discourses*, by S. Kierkegaard, published.
October 16	Moves from Nørregade 230 (now 38) to house at Nytorv 2, Copenhagen.

1845

April 29	*Three Discourses on Imagined Occasions*, by S. Kierkegaard, published.
April 30	*Stages on Life's Way*, edited by Hilarius Bogbinder, published.
May 13–24	Journey to Berlin.
May 29	*Eighteen Edifying Discourses*, by S. Kierkegaard, published.

1846

January 2	First attack on S. K. in *The Corsair*.
January 10	S. K.'s reply by Frater Taciturnus in *The Fatherland*.

February 27	*The Concluding Unscientific Postscript*, by Johannes Climacus, published.
March 30	*A Literary Review* [*The Present Age* is part of this work], by S. Kierkegaard, published.
May 2–16	Visit to Berlin.

1847

March 13	*Upbuilding Discourses in Various Spirits*, by S. Kierkegaard, published.
September 29	*Works of Love*, by S. Kierkegaard, published.
December 24	Sells house on Nytorv.

1848

January 28	Leases apartment at Rosenborggade and Tornebuskgade 152 for April occupancy.
April 26	*Christian Discourses*, by S. Kierkegaard, published.
November	Finishes *The Point of View for My Work as an Author* (Published posthumously in 1859 by S. K.'s brother Peter Christian Kierkegaard.)
	"Armed Neutrality," by S. Kierkegaard, written toward the end of 1848 and the beginning of 1849 but not published.

1849

| May 14 | Second edition of *Either/Or* and *The Lilies of the Field and the Birds of the Air*, by S. Kierkegaard, published. |

May 19	Two *Minor Ethical-Religious Treatises*, by H. H., published.
July 30	*The Sickness Unto Death*, by Anti-Climacus, published.
November 13	*Three Discourses at the Communion on Friday*, by S. Kierkegaard, published.

1850

April 18	Moves to Nørregade 43, Copenhagen.
September 27	*Training in Christianity*, by Anti-Climacus, published.
December 20	*An Edifying Discourse*, by S. Kierkegaard, published.

1851

August 7	*On My Work as an Author* and *Two Discourses at the Communion on Fridays*, by S. Kierkegaard, published.
September 10	*For Self-Examination*, by S. Kierkegaard, published.

1851–52

Judge for Yourself, by S. Kierkegaard, written. Published posthumously in 1876.

1854

January 30	Bishop Mynster dies.
April 15	H. Martensen named bishop.
December 18	S. K. begins polemic against Bishop Martensen in *The Fatherland*.

1855

January–May	Polemic continues.
May	*This Must Be Said; So Let It Now Be Said*, by S. Kierkegaard, published.
	Publishes the first number of *The Moment*.
June 16	*Christ's Judgment on Official Christianity*, by S. Kierkegaard, published.
September 3	*The Unchangeableness of God*, by S. Kierkegaard, published.
September 25	Ninth and last number of *The Moment* published; number 10 published posthumously. S. K. writes his last entry in his journals.
October 2	Enters Frederik's Hospital.
November 11	Dies.
November 18	Is buried.

The Quotable Kierkegaard

Figure 1. Kierkegaard portrait.
Drawing by Niels Christian Kierkegaard, ca. 1840. Photograph.
Royal Library, Copenhagen.

AUTOBIOGRAPHICAL

One thought succeeds another. No sooner is it thought and I want to write it down, than there is a new one: hold onto it, seize it, madness, insanity!

JN, vol. 1, Journal CC: 21, p. 198

I really hate these half-learned robbers. When I am at a social gathering, how often I have taken pains to sit down to talk with some old spinster who lives to tell family stories, listening with the greatest seriousness to everything she can prattle about.

JN, vol. 1, Journal CC: 23, p. 199

I prefer to talk with old ladies who retail family nonsense; next with the insane—and last of all with very reasonable people.

JN, vol. 1, Journal CC: 24, p. 199

[W]hy I so much prefer autumn to spring is that in the autumn one looks at heaven—in the spring at the earth.

JN, vol. 1, Journal DD: 74, p. 236

Figure 2. Kierkegaard family home.
Photograph, undated, Museum of Copenhagen.

I think that if ever I do become an earnest Christian, my deepest shame will be that I did not become one before, that I first wanted to try everything else.

JN, vol. 1, Journal DD: 89, p. 240

What does the soul find so invigorating about *reading folk tales*? When I am tired of everything and "full of days," fairy-tales are for me always the revitalizing bath that proves so refreshing.

JN, vol. 1, Journal DD: 94, p. 241

Again such a long time has passed in which I have been unable to collect myself for the least thing—I must now make another little shot at it.

Poul Møller is dead.

JN, vol. 1, Journal DD: 96, p. 243

There is an *indescribable joy* that glows through us just as inexplicably as the apostle's unmotivated exclamation: "Rejoice, and again I say, Rejoice."—Not a joy over this or that, but a full-bodied shout of the soul "with mouth and lip and heart so deep": "I rejoice at my joy, of, in, with, at, upon, by, and with my joy"—a heavenly refrain which as though suddenly interrupts our other songs, a joy which like a breath of air cools and refreshes, a puff from the trade winds that blow across the plains of Mamre to the eternal mansions.

JN, vol. 1, Journal DD: 113, pp. 245–46

How I thank you, Father in heaven, for having kept here on earth for a time like the present when my need for it can be so great, an earthly father who, as I so very much hope, will with your help have greater joy in being my father the second time than he had the first.

JN, vol. 1, Journal DD: 116, p. 246

Grasping childhood is like grasping a beautiful region as one rides in a carriage looking backward; one only becomes properly aware of the beauty at that moment, at that very instant when it begins to disappear, and all I have left of that happy time is *crying like a child.*

JN, vol. 1, Journal DD: 122[a], p. 248

My father died on Wednesday, the 8th, at 2:00 a.m. I did so earnestly desire that he should live a few years more, and I regard his death as the last sacrifice his love made for me, because he has not died from me but *died for me*, so that something might still come of me.

JN, vol. 1, Journal DD: 126, p. 249

The pity about me is that my life, my states of mind, always follow two declensions, in which not only the suffixes become different but the whole word is changed.

JN, vol. 1, Journal DD: 197, p. 267

I am so unhappy right now that I am indescribably happy in my dreams.

JN, vol. 2, Journal EE: 59[a], p. 22

All of existence makes me anxious, from the smallest fly to the mysteries of the Incarnation; I find everything inexplicable, myself most of all; everything is infected, myself most of all.

JN, vol. 2, Journal EE: 64, p. 23

I say of my grief what the Englishman says of his house: my grief is my castle.

JN, vol. 2, Journal EE: 65, p. 23

God in Heaven, let me really feel my nothingness, not so as to despair over it, but so as to feel the greatness of your goodness all the more strongly.

JN, vol. 2, Journal EE: 67, p. 24

These days my life feels rather like that of a chess piece, when the opponent says: that piece cannot be moved—like a useless bystander, since my time has not yet come.

JN, vol. 2, Journal EE: 76, p. 26

Strangely enough, there is something that has often made me anxious: that the life I was living wasn't my own but quite identical with that of another definite person, without my being able to prevent it, and I only discovered it whenever it had been lived through up to a certain point.

JN, vol. 2, Journal EE: 84, p. 28

I shall now, for a season, for some miles in time, plunge *underground* like the Guadalquivir; to be sure, I shall come up again!

JN, vol. 2, Journal EE: 128, p. 42

The reason why my progress through life is so uncertain is that my front legs (hopes, etc.) were weakened in my early youth by being overexercised.

JN, vol. 2, Journal EE: 141, p. 44

I stand like a *solitary* spruce, egoistically self-enclosed and pointing toward what is higher, casting no shadow, and only the wood dove builds its nest in my branches.

JN, vol. 2, Journal FF: 54, p. 79

Every flower of my heart turns into a frost flower.

JN, vol. 2, Journal FF: 73, p. 83

My ideas suffer the same fate as do parents who, though they bear healthy children, forget to have them christened in time; then subterranean beings come and put a changeling in place of the child (what is lacking is not the natural element, but solicitous care and development).

JN, vol. 2, Journal FF: 74, p. 84

It seems to me as if I were a galley slave chained to death; every time life stirs, the chain rattles and death makes everything wither away—*and it happens every moment.*

JN, vol. 2, Journal FF: 79, p. 84

My ideas and their elaboration are like the biting of fish during certain months of the year—they nibble. There are plenty of bites, but no fish.

JN, vol. 2, Journal FF: 84, p. 85

I am a Janus bifrons: with one face I laugh, with the other I weep.

JN, vol. 2, Journal FF: 93, p. 86

When at times there is such a racket in my head that it seems as if my cranium has been lifted up, as when gnomes lift a mountain up a bit, celebrating and making merry inside.

JN, vol. 2, Journal FF: 181, p. 101

After my death no one will find in my papers (this is my consolation) the least information about what has *really* filled my life, find *that* script in my innermost being that explains everything, and which often, for me, makes what the world would call trifles into events of immense importance, and which I too consider of no significance once I take away the secret note that explains it.

JN, vol. 2, Journal JJ: 95, p. 157

Had I faith I would have stayed with Regine. Praise and thanks be to God, I have now understood it. I have been on the point of losing my mind these days.

JN, vol. 2, Journal JJ: 115, p. 164

I was born in 1813, the wrong fiscal year, in which so many other bad banknotes were put into circulation, and my life seems best compared to one of them. There is something of greatness about me, but because of the poor state of the market I am not worth much. And at times a banknote like that became a family's misfortune.

JN, vol. 2, Journal JJ: 198, p. 188

The way it is with my feelings is like an Englishman who got into financial difficulty; even though he had a hundred-pound note, there was no one there who could change it.

JN, vol. 2, Journal JJ: 245, p. 200

There is a bird called the rainseer and that is what I am like; in our times when a storm starts brewing, individuals of my sort turn up.

JN, vol. 2, Journal JJ: 391, p. 250

My idea is now to qualify myself for the priesthood[.] For several months I have prayed to God to help me along, for it has long been clear to me that I ought not to continue as an author, which is something I want to be entirely or not at all. That's also why I haven't begun anything new while doing the proof-reading, except for the little review of *Two Ages*, which is, once more, concluding.

JN, vol. 2, Journal JJ: 415, p. 257

How dreadful the thought of that man who once, as a small boy tending sheep on the Jutland heath, in much suffering, starving and exhausted, stood up on a hill and cursed God—and that man was unable to forget it when he was 82 years old.

JN, vol. 2, Journal JJ: 416, p. 257

I am always accused of using long parentheses. Reading for my examination is the longest parenthesis I have experienced.

JN, vol. 3, Notebook 5: 19, p. 181

Next to taking off every stitch of clothing, owning nothing in the world, not the least little thing, and then hurling myself into the water, nothing pleases me more than speaking a foreign language, preferably a living one, in order to become quite foreign to myself.

JN, vol. 3, Notebook 7: 11, p. 205

My doubt is frightful.—Nothing can stop me—it is a hunger of damnation, I can consume every sort of reasoning, every consolation, every comfort—I overrun all resistance at a speed of 10,000 miles a second.

JN, vol. 3, Notebook 7: 17, p. 206

In addition to the rest of my numerous circle of acquaintances—with whom I generally have a rather superficial relationship—I have one more intimate confidante: my melancholia; and in the midst of my joy, in the midst of my work, she beckons to me, calling me away, even though I remain present in body; she is the most faithful lover whom I have known, and what wonder, then, that I must be instant[ly] ready to follow.

JN, vol. 3, Notebook 7: 28, p. 209

How great is a woman's devotion.—But the curse hanging over me is that I never dare let any one become deeply and intimately attached to me.

JN, vol. 3, Notebook 8: 15, p. 224

I cannot be quit of this relationship, for I cannot poetize it; the moment I want to poetize it, I am immediately possessed by an anxiety, an impatience which wants to resort to action.

JN, vol. 3, Notebook 8: 18, p. 225

But it is undeniably an education to be situated as I am in a small city like Copenhagen. To work to the utmost of my abilities, almost to the point of despair, with profound agony in my soul and much inner suffering, to pay out money in order to publish books— and then to have literally fewer than 10 people who read them through properly, while university students and other writers find it convenient to depict the writing of a large book as something close to ridiculous.

JN, vol. 4, Journal NB: 18, p. 15

If only I could make myself become a priest. After all, however much my present life has gratified me, out there, in quiet activity, granting myself a bit of literary productivity in my free moments, I would breathe more easily.

JN, vol. 4, Journal NB: 19, pp. 16–17

To be the greatest philosopher in Denmark borders on satire—something like being the greatest—let's think— the greatest of all the traveling theater troupes one has seen—in Odense. Or, as when P.L. Møller praised my polemic against Heiberg—"that it was the wittiest of all the things that had been written against Heiberg."

JN, vol. 4, Journal NB: 32, p. 32

I am in the deepest sense an unhappy individual who, from my earliest days, has been nailed fast to one or another suffering that verged on madness and that must have its deeper origin in a misrelation between my mind and my body—because (and this is both remarkable and an infinite encouragement to me) it has no relation to my spirit, which on the contrary, perhaps because of the tension between my mind and my body, has been granted an unusual resilience.

JN, vol. 4, Journal NB: 34, pp. 33–34

I seem to be fated never to be capable of being understood by others with respect to the decisive elements of my life. What would never occur to anyone is precisely what is decisive for me. When one lives as strenuous a life as I do, the total misunderstanding is in a certain sense an agony.

JN, vol. 4, Journal NB: 35, p. 36

I really did imagine that I understood a little something about human beings; but the longer I live, the more I realize that we absolutely do not understand one another.

JN, vol. 4, Journal NB: 71, p. 61

With respect to spelling, I submit unconditionally to authority (Molbech); it never occurs to me to want to correct him, because I know that I lack expertise in this area, which is why I willingly admit that in this respect every reasonably decent Danish author is perhaps more careful about this than I am.

With punctuation matters are different. Here I submit unconditionally to no one, and I doubt very much that there is any Danish author who could compete with me in this respect.

JN, vol. 4, Journal NB: 146, p. 98

Now, Andersen can tell the fairy tale about the "Galoshes of Good Fortune," but I can tell the fairy tale about the shoe that pinches. Or rather, I could tell it, though precisely because I will not tell it but conceal it in profound silence, I am able to tell quite a few other things.

JN, vol. 4, Journal NB: 156, p. 103

My work is of such a nature that it can only be understood after my death, but this coincides with my idea of penance.

JN, vol. 4, Journal NB2: 9, p. 139

I suffered indescribable and unrelenting injustice at the hands of those who continually construed as pride what was intended only to keep the secret of my melancholia. But, to be sure, I have achieved what I wished, for scarcely a soul has ever felt sympathy for me.

JN, vol. 4, Journal NB2: 71, p. 169

What I lack is the bodily energy—to loaf; what I have is intellectual energy, and the only thing one can do with that is work.

JN, vol. 4, Journal NB2: 87, p. 175

From earliest childhood, an arrow of grief has been embedded in my heart. As long as it remains there, I am ironic—if it is drawn out, I will die.

JN, vol. 4, Journal NB2: 92, p. 177

When one is immersed in one's own thoughts and thus on the way to forgetting actuality, it is remarkable how one is called back, as happened to me today, by a peddler woman's cry: Cherries here, 6 shillings, cherries here for 6 shillings. What really brought me back was not just that cry—but that familiar voice! The memory comes from my earliest childhood; only in more recent years she has changed a bit, her mouth has become a bit crooked, which somewhat affects her pronunciation of the word "shilling."

JN, vol. 4, Journal NB2: 112, p. 183

Until now I have protected myself against my melancholia with intellectual labor that keeps it at bay. Now—in the faith that God in forgiveness has forgotten the portion of guilt there is within it—I must myself try to forget it, though not through distraction, not by distancing myself from it, but in God, so that when I think of God, I must think that he has forgotten it, and thus myself learn to dare to forget it in forgiveness.

JN vol. 4, Journal NB2: 136, p. 194

And this is why not only my writings but indeed my life, the intriguing secret of the whole machinery, will one day be studied and studied. I dare go so far as to guarantee that there is hardly a diplomat with as good an overview of an age, even though he stands on the street and perceives every detail.

JN, vol. 4, Journal NB3: 22, p. 256

Had I not been of independent means, I would have gotten along well with my contemporaries. First of all, I wouldn't have had the time for large and thematically unified works; my achievements would have been like those of other men. That's how to be loved. They would have been trivialities—then they'd be read.

JN, vol. 4, Journal NB4: 14, p. 294

What my father said about me is true: "nothing will come of you as long as you have money." He spoke prophetically; he thought I would drink it and dream it away. But it didn't go quite that far. No, but with my sharp mind, and my melancholia, and then with money, oh, what favorable conditions for developing all the torments of self-torture in my heart.

JN, vol. 4, Journal NB4: 152, p. 357

I owe everything to my father from the very beginning. When, melancholic as he was, he saw melancholia in me, his plea to me was: See to it that you truly love Jesus Christ.

JN, vol. 4, Journal NB5: 65, p. 400

How true, then, are those words that I have so often said of myself, that as Scheherazade saved her life by telling tales, I save my life or keep myself alive by producing.

JN, vol. 5, NB8: 36, p. 167

Therefore my life is indeed also a bit of an offense: what is offensive is that it does at least approximate expressing that an idea does in fact exist. The lives of others express that there exist well-paid, excellent livings, titles, and ranks: what could be offensive about this?—no, that is truth and wisdom.

JN, vol. 6, Journal NB12: 55, p. 169

Sometimes I find it edifying to consider that the thorn or barb I have in the flesh, the suffering of which I patiently strive to bear—that this is exactly what will become, or what will help me to become a thorn in the eye of the world.

JN, vol. 6, Journal NB12: 152, p. 239

In referring to my activity as an author . . . I am like a voice, but I always have one more listener than speakers generally have: myself.

JN, vol. 6, Journal NB14: 103, p. 411

The *category* of my work is *to make people aware* of Christianity, but that is why it is always said: I'm not Christian—for otherwise there is confusion. My task is in the true sense of the term to deceive people into the religious obligation that they have cast off. But I have no authority. Instead of authority, I employ precisely the opposite: I say, The whole affair is my upbringing.

JN, vol. 6, Journal NB14: 31, p. 366

I have just now come from a gathering where I was the life of the party; witticisms flowed out of my mouth;

everybody laughed, admired me—but I left, yes, the dash ought to be as long as the radii of the earth's orbit _____

_____

and I wanted to shoot myself.

JP, vol. 5, no. 5141, p. 69

Then it was that the great earthquake occurred, the frightful upheaval which suddenly drove me to a new infallible principle for interpreting all the phenomena.

Then I surmised that my father's old-age was not a divine blessing, but rather a curse, that our family's exceptional intellectual capacities were only for mutually harrowing one another; then I felt the stillness of death deepen around me, when I saw in my father an unhappy man who would survive us all, a memorial cross on the grave of all his personal hopes.

JP, vol. 5, no. 5430, pp. 140–41

All I have is my life, which I promptly stake every time a difficulty appears. Then it is easy to dance, for the thought of death is a good dancing partner, my dancing partner.

PF, p. 8

By no means do I have faith. By nature I am a shrewd fellow, and shrewd people always have great difficulty in making the movement of faith, but I do not attribute per se any *worth to the difficulty that brought the shrewd person further in the overcoming of it than to the point at which the simplest and most unsophisticated person arrives more easily.*

   FT, p. 32

I am no fool who believes that the world becomes better because it praises me or, worse, because it censures me. . . .

   COR, p. 202

[W]hat I in truth am as an author, that I am and was a religious author, that my whole authorship pertains to Christianity, to the issue: becoming a Christian, with direct and indirect polemical aim at that enormous illusion, Christendom, or the illusion that in such a country all are Christians of sorts.

   PV, p. 23

And here I sit. Outside, everything is in commotion, nationalism sweeps everyone away; everyone talks of sacrificing life and limb, and is perhaps willing to do so, but supported by the omnipotence of opinion. And I sit in a tranquil room (—I will clearly soon be of no importance in the national cause—). I know only one danger—the danger of religiosity. But no one worries about that.

   JN, vol. 4, Journal NB4: 118, p. 346

If my melancholia has misled me in any way, it must be by having led me to want to view as guilt and sin what perhaps was only unhappy suffering, spiritual trial. In one sense, this is the most frightful misunderstanding, that is, it was the signal for almost insane anguish; but even if I have gone too far in this direction, it has nonetheless served me well.

JN, vol. 5, Journal NB8: 113, p. 201

OBSERVATIONS

Childhood is life's paradigmatic part; manhood its syntax.

JN, vol. 1, Journal AA: 30, p. 40

This is the road we all must travel—over the Bridge of Sighs into eternity.

JN, vol. 1, Journal CC: 19, p. 198

Sometimes something happens that in every way corresponds on the spiritual level with that vegetative, digestive dropping-off into a feeling of pleasant recuperation.

JN, vol. 1, Journal DD: 30, p. 222

Beware false prophets who come to you in wolves' clothing but inwardly are sheep—i.e., the phrasemongers.

JN, vol. 1, Journal DD: 66, p. 234

There is nothing more dangerous for someone, nothing more paralyzing, than a kind of isolating fixation

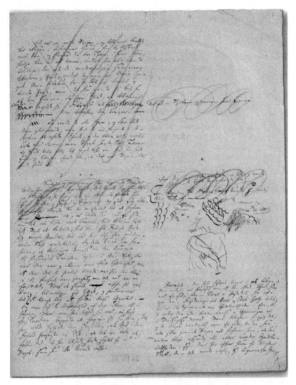

FIGURE 3. An aphorism on an undated strip of
paper, presumably from May 1835.
From the Royal Library, Copenhagen, A pk. 1.

on oneself, in which world history, human life, society—in short everything—disappears and, in an
egoistic circle . . . one constantly sees only one's own
navel.

JN, vol. 1, Journal DD: 76, p. 237

Presentiment is the earthly life's nostalgia for something higher, for the *lucidity* which man must have had in his paradisial life.

JN, vol. 1, Journal DD: 80, p. 238

Fixed ideas are like cramps e.g. in the foot—the best remedy for them is to trample on them.

JN, vol. 1, Journal DD: 115, p. 246

May our talk not be like the flower which today stands in the meadow and tomorrow is thrown into the furnace . . .

JN, vol. 1, Journal DD: 182, p. 263

The life of every individual also has its Genesis and then its *Exodus* (its exit into the world), its Leviticus, when the mind turns toward heaven, its Numbers, when one begins to count the years, its Deuteronomy.

JN, vol. 1, Journal DD: 190, p. 265

Woodland looks best from a distance, it is then an interesting mystery; seen from close up it is a riddle that has been solved; water, on the other hand, is a deep truth that becomes more interesting the further into it one peers, and the least drop of water has the same influence on the observant spirit, so that, unlike trees, one doesn't need great quantities.

JN, vol. 2, Journal EE: 109, p. 37

Abstract concepts are as invisible as a straight line, they are only visible when they are made concrete.

JN, vol. 2, Journal EE: 127, p. 42

The most agreeable, the most refreshing conversation is still that which is carried on by the trees . . .

JN, vol. 2, Journal EE: 136, p. 43

[N]ot the laughter which is the playmate of pain, that's not what I want; still less the wohlfeile syrupy smile, I don't want that at all—but the smile that is the first fruits of blessedness.

JN, vol. 2, Journal EE: 137, p. 42

There are many people who arrive at answers in life just like schoolboys; they cheat their teacher by copying the answer out of the arithmetic book without having worked the problem out themselves.

JN, vol. 2, Journal FF: 31, p. 75

"Everything that is human lies, hope as well as despair," a quotation I read in an old devotional work.

JN, vol. 2, Journal FF: 80, p. 84

Life can only be interpreted after it has been lived, just as it was only after he was resurrected that Christ began to interpret the Scriptures, showing how they taught about him.

JN, vol. 2, Journal FF: 122, p. 91

It takes moral courage to grieve; it takes religious courage to be joyful.

JN, vol. 2, Journal HH: 4, p. 120

Consciousness presupposes itself, and to ask about its origin is an idle question that is just as captious as that ancestor: What came first, the tree or the seed?

JN, vol. 2, Journal JJ: 60, p. 147

The more a person is able to forget, the more metamorphoses his life can have; the more he is able to remember, the more divine his life becomes.

JN, vol. 2, Journal JJ: 92, p. 157

The most dreadful that can happen to someone is that he becomes comical to himself in what is essential, e.g., that he discovers that the content of his feelings is nonsense.

JN, vol. 2, Journal JJ: 169, p. 180

Indeed, it can also be healthy to keep a wound open: a healthy and open wound; sometimes it is worst when it heals over.

JN, vol. 2, Journal JJ: 304, p. 217

[O]bjective thinking is not the least bit concerned about the thinker, and it finally becomes so objective that it thinks like the customs officer who was only concerned with writing—the others were concerned with reading.

JN, vol. 2, Journal JJ: 344, p. 233

The cowardly dogs, which do not bite, bark right away when they see a stranger; when he has gone past they fall silent. The dangerous dogs keep quite still when one walks past them; they follow a couple of steps behind, bark once or twice, then they bite. This is how it is with human beings and the impression made upon them by life's events: The lower sorts bark right away—the more serious ones follow behind slowly and store everything away.

JN, vol. 2, Journal JJ: 351, pp. 235–36

It is quite curious: naturally the life of a little insignificant thing is viewed with contempt, and is overlooked by all intelligent people; in return, the little insignificant thing sometimes takes revenge, for when a man goes mad it is almost always over some little insignificant thing.

JN, vol. 2, Journal JJ: 388, p. 249

As there are plants which do not merely bear their beneficial fruit but also purify and enrich the soil in which they grow, so that far from exhausting its fertility, they enrich it—so it is with every good effort; it not only bears its fruit but also purifies the soil of the mind.

JN, vol. 2, Journal JJ: 394, p. 251

And when you had become truly weary of the world, when you wanted to give vent to your passion in a single proverb, then perhaps you said: The world passeth away, and the lust thereof. But at the same instant your soul was reminded that there was an old proverb, and you involuntarily came to repeat what you next remembered from childhood: the word of the Lord endureth forever. At first you said it perfunctorily, but in the end it came to be everything to you.

JN, vol. 2, Journal JJ: 517, p. 288

When a person, gone astray to the point of perdition, is at the point of downfall, then these are the last words and the sign: Something better in me is, after all, being destroyed. As bubbles rise from a drowning man, this is the sign—then he sinks. Just as reserve can become a person's downfall, because he will not articulate what is hidden, so too the uttering of those words: the downfall, because simply saying them expresses that he has become so objective to himself that he dares to speak of his own ruin as of something decided . . .

JN, vol. 2, Journal JJ: 432, p. 262

Somewhere in Engeland [*sic*] there is a gravestone with only these words on it: The Unhappiest Man. I could imagine someone reading it and thinking there was no one buried there but that it was intended for him.

JN, vol. 3, Notebook 5: 24, p. 182

On the road to Aarhus I saw a most amusing sight: two cows roped together came cantering past us, the one frisking about with a jovial swing to its tail, the other, as it appeared, more prosaic and quite in despair at having to take part in the same movements.—Aren't most marriages so arranged?

JN, vol. 3, Notebook 6: 33, p. 197

There is indeed an equilibrium in the world. To one God gave the joys, to the other the tears and permission every once in a while to rest in his embrace;—and yet the divine reflects itself far more beautifully in the tear-dimmed eye, just as the *rain*bow is more beautiful than the clear blue sky.

JN, vol. 3, Notebook 6: 34, p. 198

[I]t takes more courage to suffer than to act, more courage to forget than to remember, and perhaps the most wonderful thing about God is that he can forget the sins of human beings.

JN, vol. 3, Notebook 7: 15, p. 205

It is after all salutary once in a while to feel that one is in God's hand and not forever sneaking around in the nooks and crannies of a familiar city where one always knows a way out.

JN, Vol. 3, Notebook 8: 8, p. 222

And when God wants to bind a person to him properly, he summons his most faithful servant, his trustiest messenger, and that is Grief, and he tells him, ["]Hurry after him, catch up with him, don't leave his side.["] . . . and no woman can cling more tenderly to what she loves than Grief [does].

JN, vol. 3, Notebook 8: 43, p. 232

Furthermore, my observations more than confirm my sense that this is how it is: If a person consistently expresses an idea, every objection raised against him will contain a self-revelation of the one who raises it.

JN, vol. 4, Journal NB: 7, p. 14

The secret of life, if one wants to get on well, is: good twaddle about what one wants to do and how one is prevented from doing it—and then, no action.

JN, vol. 4, Journal NB: 18, p. 27

Fundamentally, the world always remains just as clever—that is, just as stupid. Thus when a man—who has been misunderstood, mocked, persecuted, ridiculed, despised by his times—has fought for a truth, the next generation discovers that he was great—and admires him.

JN, vol. 4, Journal NB: 37, p. 39

Genuine magnanimity can never be rewarded in the world, quite simply because if this so-called magnanimous action is such that the times are immediately able to understand that it is magnanimous, then it is not true magnanimity in the highest sense, for of course it has its reward.

JN, vol. 4, Journal NB: 38, p. 40

Pascal says that this is why it is so difficult to believe, because it is so difficult to obey.

JN, vol. 4, Journal NB: 40, p. 41

Human envy will finally come to abolish every essential distinction, replacing it with tyrannical arbitrariness.

JN, vol. 4, Journal NB: 43, p. 43

Every person would in fact be infinitely strong if he did not need to use 2/3 of his energy in discovering his task. This is why the child has so much energy, because the father poses the task and the child must merely obey.

JN, vol. 4, Journal NB: 60, p. 51

All knowledge has something captivating about it, but on the other hand it also transforms the entire state of the knower's mind.

JN, vol. 4, Journal NB: 70, p. 60

If a maidservant asked an astronomer what time it was, he would answer, for example, It is 12 o'clock. If a businessman asked him this, he would say, Just yesterday, when I raised the flag, I set my own watch, so I know it is exactly 12 o'clock. But if an astronomer who wanted to make an observation asked him this, he would say, It is 12 o'clock, 1 minute, 37 seconds, and several decimals. He would have told the truth in all 3 cases. What he said to the maidservant was by no means untrue. That is the way simplicity and scholarship relate to one another.

JN, vol. 4, Journal NB: 72, p. 62

Even the art of printing books is an almost satirical invention, for good Lord, it has certainly become clear that there are only so many who actually have anything to communicate. Thus this great discovery has helped broadcast all the nonsense that would otherwise have been stillborn.

JN, vol. 4, Journal NB: 73, pp. 62–63

Just as one can determine the time of day by determining an object's relation to its shadow, so can one determine a person's maturity by this ratio: how close does he think he is to what is highest.

JN, vol. 4, Journal NB: 167, p. 106

"The good shepherd lays down his life for the sheep." This seems so peaceful, as everything does from a distance. One imagines the sheep gathered round the shepherd, and then the wolf comes. Alas, but suppose it was the sheep themselves who were so foolish as to side with the wolf about killing the shepherd.

JN, vol. 4, Journal NB: 183, pp. 111–12

Children play soldier, in times of peace people play war, and most people play at religion.

JN, vol. 4, Journal NB2: 36, p. 153

Most people are subjective toward themselves and objective toward all others, sometimes horribly objective—ah, the task is precisely to be objective in relation to oneself and subjective in relation to all others.

JN, vol. 4, Journal NB2: 57, p. 162

When a child in a dark room waits for the door to be opened and for the whole anticipated glory to appear, the room remains as dark, even to the last second before the door is opened, as it was to begin with. Insofar as the parents have no agreement with the child as to how long he must wait, neither does he know whether a long stretch of time remains. But one thing is sure—the second the door is opened, the glory will be revealed.

JN, vol. 4, Journal NB2: 79, p. 172

Daily worries, daily derision year in and year out, are far worse than any catastrophe, because, among other things, this always looks like nothing to an outside observer.

JN, vol. 4, Journal NB2: 80, p. 172

Money is the numerator, mercy the denominator. But, when all is said and done, the denominator is surely the more important.

JN, vol. 4, Journal NB2: 96, p. 178

It can be readily conceded that everyone who can beget children can also bring up their young (just like animals), but bringing up human beings is a very rare gift. . . . There is perhaps no situation and no tendency in which the confusion of the times will become so laughable as in the business of bringing up children. In the next generation the parents themselves will probably be so mediocre that they themselves will very much need upbringing—and it is they who are supposed to assist the schoolmaster in bringing up the children.

JN, vol. 4, Journal NB2: 144, p. 198

When a ship is to sail out of the harbor, they first cast out an end [of rope] that is rowed out by a couple of sailors in a boat, made fast to a piling, and the ship is pulled from that point. And when a human life is to begin properly, an end must also be cast out—that is, there must be a dead person who assists in getting life going. Every existence that does not have the assistance of a beloved dead person remains an insignificant existence or one that is great in a merely worldly sense.

JN, vol. 4, Journal NB2: 185, p. 213

Most people prefer to have two advisers, one for the hour of danger, when they are afraid—and then, when things go well again, then they would prefer not to have anything to do with him, because the sight of him reminds them of how weak they were, and now they prefer to imagine that they have triumphed by dint of their own strength—not by God's.

JN, vol. 4, Journal NB2: 251, p. 234

There's something far more compassionate in gray weather than in sunshine, it is like the development of the theme that something can be made even of insignificant things, yes, of things that have been thrown away. And gray weather puts on a more beautiful appearance the more one looks at it.

JN, vol. 4, Journal NB3: 25, p. 257

Augustine has said it so well: Certainly God has promised you forgiveness—but he has not promised you the next day.

JN, vol. 4, Journal NB3: 56, p. 273

Imagine a young person and how he might wish *to live*—but let us then give a test. Imagine someone dying, how he might wish *to have lived*: You will find that you come to the opposite result. Who is right, then? Really it is the one who is dying. For the youth wishes for life (for these 70 years); the one dying wishes for eternity or wishes that he had lived for the sake of eternity.

JN, vol. 4, Journal NB4: 61, p. 316

What is dangerous about the creeping villainy is that it takes considerable imagination and considerable dialectical abilities to be able to detect it at the moment and see what it is. Well, neither of these features [imagination or dialectical ability] are prominent in most people—and so the villainy creeps forward just a little bit each day, unnoticed.

JN, vol. 4, Journal NB5: 58, p. 397

The best proof for the immortality of the soul, for the existence of God, etc. is really the impression one gets of this in one's childhood and is thus the proof that, unlike those many learned and high-falutin' proofs, could be put like this: It is certainly true, because my father told it to me.

JN, vol. 4, Journal NB5: 114, p. 418

Oh, when they preach on Job, they are always in a hurry to get to the end, to the fact that he gets everything back again, double. To me it seems strange to preach about this. For isn't it true that as soon as this happens, you can certainly get yourself back on your feet and accept it—see, that's why I prefer to preach about the time preceding it.

JN, vol. 5, Journal NB6: 40, p. 30

To reduplicate is to be what one says. Human beings are therefore infinitely better served by someone who does not speak in all-too-lofty tones but who is what he says.

JN, vol. 5, Journal NB6: 57, p. 39

The person who is *unable* to seduce people, is not *able* to save them, either.

JN, vol. 5, Journal NB8: 8, p. 154

One solitary person cannot help or save an age; he can only make it clear that it is on its way to a downfall.

JN, vol. 5, Journal NB10: 93, p. 314

The essential thinker always states an issue in its most extreme form; this is precisely what is brilliant—and only a few can follow him. Then the professor comes; he takes away the "paradox"—a great many people, almost the entire multitude, can understand him, and then people think that now the truth has become truer! ... Every essential thinker can only view the professor comically.

JN, vol. 6, Journal NB12: 32, p. 161

And therefore—oh, wonderful love of Providence, which has provided every animal with one or another means of defense—thus, too, does Providence make every more profound nature silent. Through silence he saves his life, in silence; saved, he possesses his blessedness.

JN, vol. 6, Journal NB12: 135, p. 226

Weeping for oneself: this is the only right place for tears. Praised be the person who can say, I myself am the only object I find worthy enough—or wretched enough—to weep for.

JN, vol. 6, Journal NB13: 19, p. 286

Just tell me how you judge your childhood and youth, and I will tell you who you are.

JN, vo. 6, Journal NB13: 28, p. 292

The dreadful thing is not that I am to suffer punishment when I have done something wrong; the dreadful thing is that I could do something wrong—and there would be no punishment.

JN, vol. 6, Journal NB13: 46, p. 305

Priests no longer concern themselves with the cure of souls; physicians now take care of that. Instead of becoming another person through conversion, one now does so through baths, spas, and the like . . .

JN, vol. 6, Journal NB14: 64, p. 386

People must indeed have lived in a far simpler fashion when they believed that God revealed his will in dreams. . . . [T]he poor opinion of dreams typical of our times is . . . connected to the spiritualism that constantly presses upon consciousness, whereas those simpler times piously believed that the unconscious life in a person was both the dominant and the most profound aspect.

JN, vol. 6, Journal NB14: 83, p. 398

And even if "the professor" happened to read this, it would not stop him, it would not prick his conscience—no, he would lecture on this, too. And even if the professor happened to read this remark, it would not stop him either—no, he would lecture on this, too. For the professor is even longer than the tapeworm which a woman was delivered of recently (200 feet according to her husband . . .

JP, vol. 6, no. 6818, p. 454

The age of making distinctions is passed. It has been vanquished by the system. In our day, whoever loves to make distinctions is regarded as an eccentric whose soul clings to something that has long since vanished.

CA, opening page

Not everyone who is stooped-shouldered is an Atlas, nor did he become such by supporting a world.

CA, p. 7

Appropriation is precisely the secret of conversation.

CA, p. 16

The subject of which psychology treats must be something in repose that remains in a restless repose, not something restless that always either produces itself or is repressed.

CA, p. 21

[T]he older and the more spiritually developed the individuality is, the less beautiful it is in sleep, whereas the child is more beautiful in sleep.

CA, p. 65

To offer witticisms about the sexual is a paltry art, to admonish is not difficult, to preach about it in such a way that the difficulty is omitted is not hard, but to speak humanly about it is an art.

CA, p. 67

Many a marriage has been profaned, and not by a stranger.

CA, p. 71

However, life is rich enough, if only one understands how to see. One need not travel to Paris and London; besides, this would be of no help if one is unable to see.

CA, p. 74

If I am anxious about a past misfortune, then this is not because it is in the past but because it may be repeated, i.e., become future.

CA, p. 91

Yet instead of learning from this how to lay hold of the eternal, we only learn how to drive ourselves, our neighbors, and the moment to death—in the pursuit of the moment. If a person could have a part just once, could lead the waltz of the moment just once—then he has lived, then he becomes the envy of the less fortunate, those who are not born but rush headlong into life, and headlong continue to rush forward, never reaching it.

CA, p. 105

Whoever has some understanding of men knows very well that sophistry always fixes upon one particular point and continually skirts the point.

CA, p. 114

In our courageous age, we dare not tell a patient that he is about to die, we dare not call the pastor lest he die from shock, and we dare not tell the patient that a few days ago a man died from the same disease.

CA, p. 121

But why do people rush around in such a terrible haste? If there is no eternity, the moment is just as long as if there were.

CA, p. 152

[I]t is often distressing to be an observer—it has the same melancholy effect as being a police officer.

R, p. 135

I went out to the café where I had gone every day the previous time to enjoy the beverage that, according to the poet's precept, when it is "pure and hot and strong and not misused," can always stand alongside that to which the poet compares it, namely, friendship. At any rate, I prize coffee.

R, pp. 169–70

I stick my finger into the world—it has no smell. Where am I? What does it mean to say: the world? What is the meaning of that word? Who tricked me into this whole thing and leaves me standing here? Who am I? How did I get into the world? Why was I not asked about it, why was I not informed of the rules and regulations but just thrust into the ranks as if I had been bought from a peddling shanghaier of human beings? How did I get involved in this big enterprise called actuality? Why should I be involved? Isn't it a matter of choice? And if I am compelled to be involved, where is the manager—I have something to say about this.

R, p. 200

But the crowd can rarely account for its judgment, has one opinion today, another tomorrow.

PC, p. 42

But it must be remembered that with regard to differences in life everyone wants to cling to his own; it is because of this fixed point, this consideration, that *human* compassion is always merely to a certain degree.

PC, p. 59

To make oneself quite literally *one with the most wretched* (and this, and this alone is *divine* compassion), this is "too much" for people, something they can shed a few emotional tears over during a quiet Sunday hour and involuntarily burst out laughing over when they see it in *actuality*.

PC, p. 59

For people are willing enough to practice compassion and self-denial, willing enough to seek after wisdom, etc., but they want to determine the criterion themselves, that it shall be to *a certain degree*.

PC, p. 60

In order truly to will the good, one must avoid even the appearance of doing it.

PC, p. 129

[I]f there is something you want to forget, then try to find something else to remember . . .

PC, p. 152

[T]he admirer . . . keeps himself personally detached; he forgets himself, forgets that what he admires in the other person is denied to him, and precisely this is what is beautiful, that he forgets himself in this way in order to admire.

PC, p. 242

And yet there is an infinite difference between an admirer and an imitator, because an imitator is, or at least strives to be, what he admires.

PC, p. 249

Above all, do not lose your desire to walk: every day I walk myself into a state of well-being and walk away from every illness; I have walked myself into my best thoughts, and I know of no thought so burdensome that one cannot walk away from it.

LD, p. 214

Take the riches away, then I can no longer be called rich; but take tomorrow away—alas, then I can no longer be called rich either.

CD, p. 27

The rich pagan, however, also has only one thought: riches. . . . Not only is he without God in the world, but wealth is his god, which attracts to itself his every thought.

CD, p. 33

Trouble and today correspond to each other; self-torment and the next day also go together.

CD, p. 71

Oh, in the customary pursuits of daily life, how easy it is, in the spiritual sense, to doze off. . . .

CD, p. 254

The present age is essentially a *sensible, reflecting age, devoid of passion, flaring up in superficial, short-lived enthusiasm and prudentially relaxing in indolence.*

TA, p. 68

Not even a suicide these days does away with himself in desperation but deliberates on this step so long and so sensibly that he is strangled by calculation, making it a moot point whether or not he can really be called a suicide, inasmuch as it was in fact the deliberating that took his life.

TA, p. 68

So ultimately the object of desire is money, but it is in fact token money, an abstraction. A young man today would scarcely envy another his capacities or his skill or the love of a beautiful girl or his fame, no, but he would envy him his money. Give me money, the young man will say, and I will be all right.

TA, p. 75

Entrapped air always becomes noxious, and the entrapment of reflection with no ventilating action or event develops censorious envy.

TA, p. 82

If an insurrection at its peak is so like a volcanic explosion that a person cannot hear himself speak, leveling at its peak is like a deathly stillness in which a person can hear himself breathe, a deathly stillness in which nothing can rise up but everything sinks down into it, impotent.

TA, p. 84

Nowadays it is possible actually to speak with people, and what they say is admittedly very sensible, and yet the conversation leaves the impression that one has been speaking with an anonymity.

TA, p. 103

[I]f one is reminded every day to forget, one never does really forget.

FSE, p. 37

[I]t takes a personality, an *I,* to look at oneself in a mirror; a wall can be seen in a mirror, but a wall cannot see itself or look at itself in a mirror. No, while reading God's Word you must incessantly say to yourself: It is I to whom it is speaking; it is I about whom it is speaking.

FSE, p. 44

It is so easy to trip the light fantastic of desire, but when, after a while, it is desire that dances with a person against his will—that is a ponderous dance.

FSE, p. 66

[W]hat one's life proclaims is a hundred thousand times more powerfully effective than what one's mouth proclaims . . .

FSE, pp. 131–32

Concepts, just like individuals, have their history and are no more able than they to resist the dominion of time, but in and through it all they nevertheless harbor a kind of homesickness for the place of their birth.

CI, p. 9

[T]he endless calculating of the circumstances of pleasure impedes and stifles pleasure itself.

CI, p. 61

Presumably it could occur to a human being to poetize himself in the likeness of the god or the god in
the likeness of himself, but not to poetize that the
god poetized himself in the likeness of a human
being.

PF, p. 36

A person lives undisturbed in himself, and then awakens the paradox of self-love as love for another, for one
missing.

PF, p. 39

[T]rying to get rid of something by sleeping is just as
useless as trying to obtain something by sleeping.

PF, p. 43

Thus, belief believes what it does not see; it does not
believe that the star exists, for that it sees, but it believes that the star has come into existence.

PF, p. 81

In one person's mouth the same words can be so full
of substance, so trustworthy, and in another person's mouth they can be like the vague whispering of
leaves.

WL, pp. 11–12

There is only one whom a person should fear, and that is God; and there is only one of whom a person should be afraid, and that is oneself.

WL, p. 15

Unchangingness is the true independence.

WL, p. 39

Even if passionate preference had no other selfishness in it, it would still have this, that consciously or unconsciously there is self-willfulness in it—unconsciously insofar as it is in the power of natural predispositions, consciously insofar as it utterly gives itself to this power and assents to it.

WL, p. 55

Whether someone savoring his arrogance and his pride openly gives other people to understand that they do not exist for him and, for the nourishment of his arrogance, wants them to feel it as he demands expressions of slavish submission from them, or whether he slyly and secretly expresses that they do not exist for him simply by avoiding any contact with them . . . — these are basically one and the same.

WL, p. 74

The yes of the promise is sleep-inducing, but the no, spoken and therefore audible to oneself, is awakening, and repentance is usually not far away.

WL, p. 93

When a man turns his back on someone and walks away, it is easy to see that he is walking away; but when a person hits upon the idea of facing one from whom he is walking away, hits upon the idea of walking backward while with appearance and glance and salutations he greets someone, giving assurances again and again that he is coming immediately or even incessantly saying, "Here I am!"—although he is moving further and further, note well, backward: then it is not very easy to become aware. And so it is also with the one who, rich in good intentions and quick to promise, moves backward further and further away from the good.

WL, p. 94

What the world actually admires as sagacity is knowledge of evil—whereas wisdom is knowledge of the good.

WL, p. 285

It is only too certain that every human being, unfortunately, has a great inclination to see his neighbor's faults and perhaps an even greater one to want to tell them. If there is nothing else, there is, alas, to use the mildest term, a kind of nervous debility that makes people very weak in this temptation . . .

WL, p. 290

That the existing subjective thinker is continually striving does not mean, however, that in a finite sense he has a goal toward which he is striving, where he would be finished when he reached it.

CUP, p. 91

Suppose a person is given the task of entertaining himself for one day and by noon is already finished with the entertainment—then his speed would indeed be of no merit. So it is also when life is the task. To be finished with life before life is finished with one is not to finish the task at all.

CUP, p. 164

Don Quixote is the prototype of the subjective lunacy in which the passion of inwardness grasps a particular fixed finite idea. But when inwardness is absent, parroting lunacy sets in, which is just as comic . . .

CUP, p. 195

Mood is like the Niger River in Africa; no one knows its source, no one knows its outlet—only its reach is known!

CUP, p. 237

I know very well that people usually admire the artist-life of a person who follows his talent without accounting to himself for what it means to be human, so that the admirer forgets him in admiration over his work of art. But I also know that the tragedy of an existing person of that sort is that he is a variant [*Differents*] and the differential is not personally reflected in the ethical.

CUP, p. 303

Every individuality of distinction always has some one-sidedness, and the one-sidedness itself can be an indirect declaration of his actual greatness, but it is not the greatness itself.

CUP, p. 349

I am well aware that if anyone nowadays were to live as a Greek philosopher, that is, would existentially express what he would have to call his life-view, be existentially absorbed in it, he would be regarded as lunatic.

CUP, p. 352

That one person can swim the channel and a second person knows twenty-four languages and a third person walks on his hands etc.—one can admire that *si placet* [if you please]. But if the person presented is supposed to be great with regard to the universal because of his virtue, his faith, his nobility, his faithfulness, his perseverance, etc., then admiration is a deceptive relation or can easily become that. What is great with regard to the universal must therefore not be presented as an object for admiration, but as a *requirement*.

CUP, p. 358

I prefer to talk with children, for one may still dare to hope that they may become rational beings; but those who have become that—good Lord!

EO,1, p. 19

I don't feel like doing anything. I don't feel like riding—the motion is too powerful; I don't feel like walking—it is too tiring; I don't feel like lying down, for either I would have to stay down, and I don't feel like doing that, or I would have to get up again, and I don't feel like doing that, either. *Summa Summarum:* I don't feel like doing anything.

EO,1, p. 20

Old age fulfills the dreams of youth. One sees this in Swift: in his youth he built an insane asylum; in his old age he himself entered it.

EO,1, p. 21

What if everything in the world were a misunderstanding; what if laughter really were weeping!

EO,1, p. 21

Alas, fortune's door does not open inward so that one can push it open by rushing at it; but it opens outward, and therefore one can do nothing about it.

EO,1, p. 23

I complain that in life it is not as in the novel, where one has hardhearted fathers and nisses and trolls to battle, and enchanted princesses to free. What are all such adversaries together compared with the pale, bloodless, tenacious-of-life nocturnal forms with which I battle and to which I myself give life and existence.

EO,1, p. 23

On the whole, I lack the patience to live. I cannot see the grass grow, and if I cannot do that, I do not care to look at it at all. My views are the superficial observations of a *"fahrender Scholastiker* [traveling scholastic]" who dashes through life in the greatest haste. It is said that our Lord satisfies the stomach before the eyes. That is not what I find: my eyes are surfeited and bored with everything, and yet I hunger.

EO,1, p. 25

People's thoughts are as thin and fragile as lace, and they themselves as pitiable as lace-making girls. The thoughts of their hearts are too wretched to be sinful. It is perhaps possible to regard it as sin for a worm to nourish such thoughts, but not for a human being, who is created in the image of God.

EO,1, p. 27

Human dignity is still acknowledged even in nature, for when we want to keep birds away from the trees we set up something that is supposed to resemble a human being, and even the remote resemblance a scarecrow has to a human being is sufficient to inspire respect.

EO,1, p. 28

The best demonstration of the wretchedness of life [*Tilværelse*] is that which is obtained through a consideration of its glory.

EO,1, p. 28

Most people rush after pleasure so fast that they rush right past it.

EO,1, p. 29

How empty and meaningless life is.—We bury a man; we accompany him to the grave, throw three spadefuls of earth on him; we ride out in a carriage, ride home in a carriage; we find consolation in the thought that we have a long life ahead of us. But how long is seven times ten years?

EO,1, p. 29

In a theater, it happened that a fire started offstage. The clown came out to tell the audience. They thought it was a joke and applauded. He told them again, and they became still more hilarious. This is the way, I suppose, that the world will be destroyed—amid the universal hilarity of wits and wags who think it is all a joke.

EO,1, p. 30

Real enjoyment consists not in what one enjoys but in the idea.

EO,1, p. 31

If I had in my service a submissive jinni who, when I asked for a glass of water, would bring me the world's most expensive wines, deliciously blended, in a goblet, I would dismiss him until he learned that the enjoyment consists not in what I enjoy but in getting my own way.

EO,1, p. 31

For me nothing is more dangerous than to recollect [*erindre*]. As soon as I have recollected a life relationship, that relationship has ceased to exist. It is said that absence makes the heart grow fonder. That is very true, but it becomes fonder in a purely poetic way.

EO,1, p. 32

To live in recollection is the most perfect life imaginable; recollection is more richly satisfying than all actuality, and it has a security that no actuality possesses. A recollected life relationship has already passed into eternity and has no temporal interest anymore.

EO,1, p. 32

My life is utterly meaningless. When I consider its various epochs, my life is like the word *Schnur* in the dictionary, which first of all means a string, and second a daughter-in-law. All that is lacking is that in the third place the world *Schnur* means a camel, in the fourth a whisk broom.

EO,1, p. 36

[M]y soul's poisonous doubt consumes everything. My soul is like the Dead Sea, over which no bird is able to fly; when it has come midway, it sinks down, exhausted, to death and destruction.

EO,1, p. 37

How dreadful boredom is—how dreadfully boring; I know no stronger expression, no truer one, for like is recognized only by like.

EO,1, p. 37

Marry, and you will regret it. Do not marry, and you will also regret it. Marry or do not marry, you will regret it either way. Whether you marry or you do not marry, you will regret it either way. Laugh at the stupidities of the world, and you will regret it; weep over them, and you will also regret it.

EO,1, p. 38

Wine no longer cheers my heart; a little of it makes me sad—much, depressed. My soul is dull and slack; in vain do I jab the spur of desire into its side; it is exhausted, it can no longer raise itself up in its royal jump.

EO,1, p. 41

Perhaps nothing ennobles a person so much as keeping a secret. It gives a person's whole life significance, which it has, of course, only for himself: it saves a person from all futile consideration of the surrounding world.

EO,1, p. 157

Boredom is the root of all evil.

EO,1, p. 285

On a secretly blushing cheek shines the glow of the heart.

EO,1, p. 378

Are you not aware that there comes a midnight hour when everyone must unmask; do you believe that life will always allow itself to be trifled with; do you believe that one can sneak away just before midnight in order to avoid it?

EO,2, p. 160

Frequently I have noticed in life that the costlier the liquid on which a person becomes intoxicated, the more difficult the cure becomes; the intoxication is more beautiful and the consequences apparently not as pernicious.

EO,2, p. 194

[T]he person who lives esthetically sees only possibilities everywhere; for him these make up the content of future time, whereas the person who lives ethically sees tasks everywhere.

EO,2, p. 251

As soon as the talent is not regarded as a calling—and if it is regarded as calling every human being has a calling—the talent is absolutely egotistic. Therefore, everyone who bases his life on a talent establishes to the best of his ability a robber-existence.

EO,2, p. 292

The phrase "to accomplish" signifies a relation between my action and something else that lies outside me. Now, it is easy to see that this relation does not lie in my power, and to that extent it is just as appropriate to say of the most talented person as of the humblest of men—that he accomplishes nothing.

EO,2, p. 295

The absolute condition for friendship is unity in a life-view. If a person has that, he will not be tempted to base his friendship on obscure feelings or on indefinable sympathies.

EO,2, p. 319

No matter how strong a person is, no person is stronger than himself.

EUD, p. 18

Without understanding how, they are in the midst of the movement of life, a link in the chain that binds a past to a later time; unconcerned about how it happens, they are carried along on the wave of the present. Reposing in the law of nature that lets a human life grow up in the world as it spreads a carpet of flowers over the earth, they go on living happy and contented amid the changes of life, and no moment desire to tear themselves free from them . . .

EUD, p. 33

[W]hat one sees depends on how one sees.

EUD, p. 59

Tell someone who your friends are, and he will know you; confide your wishes to him, and he will understand you; not only is your soul manifest in the wish, but inasmuch as the wish craftily betrays to him your inner state he sees through you in another way also.

EUD, p. 253

Who has forgotten the priceless enjoyment of childhood—wishing, which is the same for the poor child and for the rich child! Who has forgotten those beautiful stories from a vanished period in which, just as in childhood, wishing is the meaning of life . . .

EUD, p. 253

[I]f he nevertheless is unwilling to be an instrument of war in the service of inexplicable drives, indeed, in the service of the world, because the world itself, the object of his craving, stimulates the drives . . . a stringed instrument in the hands of inexplicable moods or, rather, in the hands of the world, because the movement of his soul is in accord with the way the world plucks its strings . . . a mirror in which he intercepts the world or, rather, the world reflects itself . . .

EUD, p. 308

From the external and visible world there comes an old adage: "Only one who works gets bread." Oddly enough, the adage does not fit the world in which it is most at home, for imperfection is the fundamental law of the external world, and here it happens again and again that he who does not work does get bread, and he who sleeps gets it even more abundantly than he who works.

FT, p. 27

What, then, is education? I believed it is the course the individual goes through in order to catch up with himself, and the person who will not go through this course is not much helped by being born in the most enlightened age.

FT, p. 46

I require every person not to think so inhumanly of himself that he does not dare to enter those palaces where the memory of the chosen ones lives or even those where they themselves live. He is not to enter rudely and foist his affinity upon them. He is to be happy for every time he bows before them, but he is to be confident, free of spirit, and always more than a charwoman, for if he wants to be no more than that, he will never get in.

FT, p. 64

But although "impractical," yet the religious is eternity's transfigured rendition of the most beautiful dream of politics.

PV, p. 103

And the ocean, like the wise man, is self-sufficient, whether it lies just like a child and amuses itself by itself with gentle ripples, like a child playing on its lips, or at midday lies, like a half-sleeping indulgent thinker, surveying everything around it, or at night it deeply ponders its own nature; whether with profound subtlety it makes itself into nothing in order to observe or it rages in its own passion. The ocean runs deep, it indeed knows what it knows; the one who runs deep always knows that . . .

UDVS, pp. 20–21

Purity of Heart Is to Will One Thing
  UDVS, p. 24

[I]nspired words are quickly forgotten in the trivialities of life.
  UDVS, p. 31

[T]here is a hope that should be killed, just as there is a lust, a craving, and a longing that should be killed—the earthly hope should be killed . . .
  UDVS, p. 116

Purity of heart—this is a metaphorical expression that compares the heart to the ocean, and why specifically to that? Because the ocean's depth is its purity, and its purity is its transparency, because the ocean is deep only when it is pure, and pure only when it is transparent.
  UDVS, p. 121

Worldly worry always seeks to lead a human being into the small-minded unrest of comparisons . . .
  UDVS, p. 188

[S]ome wear the medal to their honor and others honor the medal by wearing it.
  UDVS, p. 199

If it is possible, if I have wasted my best time without experiencing anything, at least teach me in so doing not to become indifferent, teach me not to seek the consolation of others in a common loss; then surely the terror of the loss may be a beginning of my healing.

TDIO, p. 22

Wonder, however, which is the beginning of all deeper understanding, is an ambivalent passion that in itself contains fear and blessedness.

TDIO, p. 24

In relation to every human being, the lowliest and the greatest, it holds true that not an angel and not legions of angels and not the horrors of the whole world can impart true wonder and true fear, but they certainly can make him superstitious.

TDIO, p. 25

Ah, it is much easier to look to the right and to the left than to look into oneself, much easier to haggle and bargain just as it is also much easier to underbid than to be silent—but the more difficult is still the one thing needful.

TDIO, p. 31

[T]he weed of corruption has the characteristic that all weeds have: it sows itself.

TDIO, p. 55

Now, just as it is true that in everyone's soul there is a longing like that erotic love the poets celebrate, so there is also in everyone the longing, a wish, that craves what might be called the guide and teacher in life, the tested person whom one can trust, the wise person who knows how to counsel, the noble person who encourages by his own example, the gifted person who has the power of eloquence and the substance of conviction, the earnest person who safeguards the appropriation.

TDIO, p. 58

There is a consolation in life, a false flatterer; there is a safeguard in life, a hypocritical deceiver—it is called postponement.

TDIO, p. 79

It is the fraudulence of sadness to be unwilling to understand that there is something else to fear than life, and therefore a consoling wisdom other than the sleep of death must be found.

TDIO, p. 81

This is the way a person always gains courage; when he fears a greater danger, he always has the courage to face a lesser one; when he is exceedingly afraid of one danger, it is as if the others did not exist at all.

SUD, pp. 8–9

As a matter of fact, in the world there is interest only in intellectual or esthetic limitation or in the indifferent (in which there is the greatest interest in the world), for the secular mentality is nothing more or less than the attribution of infinite worth to the indifferent.

SUD, p. 33

If I have ventured wrongly, well, then life helps me by punishing me. But if I have not ventured at all, who helps me then?

SUD, p. 34

There is a story about a peasant who went barefooted to town with enough money to buy himself a pair of stockings and shoes and to get drunk, and in trying to find his way home in his drunken state, he fell asleep in the middle of the road. A carriage came along, and the driver shouted to him to move or he would drive over his legs. The drunken peasant woke up, looked at his legs and, not recognizing them because of the shoes and stockings, said: "Go ahead, they are not my legs."

SUD, p. 53

No, whatever a man may arrive at as a matter of course, whatever things may come as a matter of course—faith and wisdom are definitely not among them.

SUD, p. 58

In antiquity as well as in the Middle Ages there was an awareness of this longing for solitude and the respect for what it means; whereas in the constant sociality of our day we shrink from solitude to the point (what a capital epigram!) that no use for it is known other than as punishment for criminals.

SUD, p. 64

To defend something is always to disparage it.

SUD, p. 87

The beginning is not that with which one begins but that to which one comes, and one comes to it backward.

WA, p. 11

[N]o one teaches joy better than one who is joyful oneself.

WA, p. 36

[S]implicity is that the teacher himself is what he is teaching.

WA, p. 38

As a subject I am to honor and obey the king with undivided soul, but I am permitted to be built up religiously by the thought that essentially I am a citizen of heaven and that if I ever meet his departed majesty there I shall not be bound in subservient obedience to him.

WA, p. 100

To honor one's father because he is exceptionally intelligent is impiety.

WA, p. 101

[P]erhaps the most dangerous temptations are those that come under the modest label of "nothing at all."

COR, p. 180

To believe the ideality on the word of another is like laughing at a joke not because one has understood it but because someone else said that it was funny.

SLW, p. 438

The *most* glorious powers are set in motion in order to get a committee set up; as soon as it is done, no one cares about the matter anymore.

TM, p. 389 (note)

Indeterminableness is the basis of dizziness . . . Therefore the remedy for dizziness is limitation; and in the spiritual sense all discipline is limitation.

BA, p. 288

Now it is certainly true that to have mood can be something very genuine and that no mortal life is so absolute that it does not know the contrasts involved therein. In a sound and healthy life, however, the mood is just an intensification of the life that ordinarily stirs and moves within a person.

CI, p. 284

In life it is very important to be on the watch for one's cue.

JN, vol. 2, Journal FF: 11, p. 70

Someone who has one thought, but an infinite one, can be borne along by it through his entire life, lightly and on wings . . .

JN, vol. 2, Journal JJ: 32, p. 141

It is said that experience makes a person wise. That is a very unreasonable thing to say. If there were nothing greater still than experience, experience would make him mad.

JN, vol. 2, Journal JJ: 57, p. 146

Do not promise never to forget . . . —no, rather turn the situation around and say, "This certainly is nothing to remember for my whole life, but I promise that I will remember it promptly this very hour, and I will keep that promise."

FSE, pp. 45–46

One of the ostensibly most respectable answers given to this "why" of marriage is: Marriage is a school for character . . .

EO,2, p. 64

What is joy, or what is it to be joyful? It is truly to be present to oneself . . .

WA, p. 39

Whatever one generation learns from another, no generation learns the essentially human from a previous one. In this respect, each generation begins primitively . . . For example, no generation has learned to love from another, no generation is able to begin at any other point than at the beginning, no later generation has a more abridged task than the previous one . . .

FT, p. 121

The art of recollecting is not easy, because in the moment of preparation it can become something different, whereas memory merely fluctuates between remembering correctly and remembering incorrectly. For example, what is homesickness? It is something remembered that is recollected. Homesickness is prompted simply by one's being absent. The art would be to be able to feel homesickness even though one is at home. This takes proficiency in illusion.

SLW, p. 13

Indeed, did Adam dare to recollect Eden; did he dare, when he saw thistles and thorns at his feet, did he dare to say to Eve: No! It was not like this in Eden. In Eden, oh, do you recollect? Did Adam dare to do this? Even less do I.

SLW, p. 350

Take a book, the poorest one written, but read it with the passion that it is the only book you will read—ultimately you will read everything out of it, that is, as much as there was in yourself . . .

SLW, p. 364

Not until the moment when there awakens in his soul a concern about what meaning the world has for him and he for the world, about what meaning everything within him by which he himself belongs to the world has for him and he therein for the world—only then does the inner being announce its presence in this *concern.*

EUD, p. 86

What is more difficult—to awaken someone who is sleeping or to awaken someone who, awake, is dreaming that he is awake?

WL, p. 5

FIGURE 4. Kierkegaard statue in front of Royal Library.
Photograph of the plaster model for the large bronze statue
in front of the Royal Library in Copenhagen.

ANXIETY

Anxiety is a qualification of dreaming spirit, as such it has its place in psychology. Awake, the difference between myself and my other is posited; sleeping, it is suspended; dreaming, it is an intimated nothing.

CA, pp. 41–42

Hence anxiety is the dizziness of freedom, which emerges when the spirit wants to posit the synthesis and freedom looks down into its own possibility, laying hold of finiteness to support itself.

CA, p. 61

As anxiety is posited in modesty, so it is present in all erotic enjoyment, and by no means because it is sinful.

CA, p. 71

Fate, then, is the nothing of anxiety.

CA, p. 97

To the extent that in every state possibility is present, anxiety is also present. Such is the case after sin is posited, for only in the good is there a unity of state and transition.

CA, p. 113

Whoever has learned to be anxious in the right way has learned the ultimate.

CA, p. 155

Anxiety is freedom's possibility, and only such anxiety is through faith absolutely educative, because it consumes all finite ends and discovers all their deceptiveness.

CA, p. 155

If, on the other hand, the speaker maintains that the great thing about him is that he has never been in anxiety, I will gladly provide him with my explanation: that is because he is very spiritless.

CA, p. 157

Deepest within every person there is nonetheless an anxiety about being alone in the world, forgotten by God, overlooked among the millions and millions in this enormous household. People keep this anxiety at bay by looking at the many people around them, who are related to them as family and friends; but the anxiety is there all the same—one scarcely dare think about how one would feel if all these were taken away.

JN, vol. 4, Journal NB2: 239, p. 230

"Let us eat and drink, because tomorrow we shall die." . . . This very remark echoes with the anxiety about the next day, the day of annihilation, the anxiety that insanely is supposed to signify joy although it is a shriek from the abyss. He is so anxious about the next day that he plunges himself into a frantic stupor in order, if possible, to forget it—and how anxious he is—is this what it means to be without care about the next day?

CD, p. 77

What is anxiety? It is the next day.

CD, p. 78

The ethical expression for what Abraham did is that he meant to murder Isaac; the religious expression is that he meant to sacrifice Isaac—but precisely in this contradiction is the anxiety that can make a person sleepless, and yet without this anxiety Abraham is not who he is.

FT, p. 30

Just as a physician might say that there very likely is not one single living human being who is completely healthy, so anyone who really knows mankind might say that there is not one single living human being who does not despair a little, who does not secretly harbor an unrest, an inner strife, a disharmony, an anxiety about an unknown something or a something he does not even dare to try to know, an anxiety about some possibility in existence or an anxiety about himself, so that, just as the physician speaks of going around with an illness in the body, he walks around with a sickness, carries around a sickness of the spirit that signals its presence at rare intervals in and through an anxiety he cannot explain.

SUD, p. 22

Despite its illusory security and tranquillity, all immediacy is anxiety and thus, quite consistently, is most anxious about nothing.

SUD, p. 25

[T]he anxiety that characterizes spiritlessness is recognized precisely by its spiritless sense of security.

    SUD, p. 44

The woman has more anxiety than the man; therefore it was she whom the serpent chose to attack, and deceived her through her anxiety.

    JN, vol.2, Journal JJ: 511a, p. 286

If a child was told that it is a sin to break one's leg, what anxiety would the child live in, and he would probably break it more often . . .

    JN, vol. 2, Journal JJ: 377, p. 245

[T]he serpent's power consists precisely of anxiety; it is not so much the cunning that is wily as the cunning that knows how to create anxiety.

    JN, vol. 6, Journal NB12: 154, p. 240

To suppose that anxiety is an imperfection merely betrays a straightlaced cowardice, since, to the contrary, the greatness of anxiety is the very prophet of the miracle of perfection, and inability to become anxious is a sign of one's being either an animal or an angel, which according to the teaching of scriptures, is less perfect than being a human being.

    JP, vol. 1, no. 97, p. 39

Just as the gospel about the lilies contains a warning to the poor against pecuniary worries, it also has a word for the corresponding kind of worry which the rich in particular usually have. "No one can add one cubit to his stature." The hypochondriacal concern that one's heart is not beating properly, that one is constipated, etc.

JP, vol. 1, no. 99, p. 40

If a person could be entirely free of anxiety, temptation would not have access to him.

JP, vol. 1, no. 102, p. 41

Anxiety is the first reflex of possibility, a glimpse, and yet a terrible sorcery.

JP, vol. 1, no. 102, p. 41

Anxiety is the vehicle by which the subject appropriates sorrow and assimilates it. Anxiety is the motive power by which sorrow penetrates a person's heart. But the movement is not swift like that of an arrow; it is consecutive; it is not once and for all, but it is continually becoming. As a passionately erotic glance craves its object, so anxiety looks cravingly upon sorrow.

EO,1, p. 154

DEPRESSION/MELANCHOLY

In addition to my other numerous acquaintances, I have one more intimate confidant—my depression. In the midst of my joy, in the midst of my work, she beckons to me, calls me aside, even though physically I remain on the spot. My depression is the most faithful mistress I have known—no wonder, then, that I return the love.

EO,1, p. 20

I have only one friend, and that is echo. Why is it my friend? Because I love my sorrow, and echo does not take it away from me. I have only one confidant, and that is the silence of night. Why is it my confidant? Because it remains silent.

EO,1, p. 33

By way of precaution, I shall promptly point out that a person can have sorrow and care—indeed, this can be so deep that it may follow him his whole life, and this can even be beautiful and true—but only through his own fault does a person become depressed.

EO,2, p. 185

What, then, is depression? It is hysteria of the spirit.

EO,2, p. 188

There is something unexplainable in depression [*Tungsind*]. A person with a sorrow or a worry knows why he sorrows or worries. If a depressed person is asked what the reason is, what it is that weighs [*tynge*] on him, he will answer: I do not know; I cannot explain it. Therein lies the limitlessness of depression.

EO,2, p. 189

But depression is sin, is actually a sin *instar omnium* [that stands for all], for it is the sin of not willing deeply and inwardly, and this is a mother of all sins.

EO,2, p. 189

It is a cowardly craving of depression to want to become dizzy in the emptiness and to seek the final diversion in this dizziness . . .

TDIO, p. 87

As a woman who is unhappy in her house spends a great deal of time at the window, so does the soul of the melancholic spend a great deal of time at the eye, seeking diversions. Another form of melancholia is that which completely closes its eye in order to darken everything around itself.

JN, vol. 4, Journal NB2: 125, p. 189

[D]epression is something real that one does not delete with the stroke of the pen.

SLW, p. 175

Precisely because he is depressed he has an abstract notion that life for others is so pleasant and happy. But what the unfamiliar is like one cannot know *in abstracto*. Here, too, is the fraudulence that is inseparable from all depression.

SLW, p. 175

Depression is my nature, that is true, but thanks be to the power who, even if it bound me in this way, nevertheless also gave me a consolation. There are animals that are only poorly armed against their enemies, but nature has provided them with a cunning by which they nevertheless are saved. I, too, was given a cunning such as this, a capacity for cunning that makes me just as strong as everyone against whom I have tested my strength. My cunning is that I am able to hide my depression; my deception is just as cunning as my depression is deep.

SLW, pp. 195–96

Everything is asleep; at this hour only the dead emerge from the grave and live their lives over again. And I am not doing even that, for since I am not dead I cannot live my life over again, and if I were dead, I could not relive it either, for, after all, I have never lived.

SLW, p. 211

Alas, why were nine months in the womb enough to make me an old man! Alas, why was I not swaddled in joy? Why was I born not only in pain but to pain? Why were my eyes opened not to what is happy but only to peer into that kingdom of sighs and to be unable to tear myself away from it?

SLW, p. 263

What is my sickness? Depression. Where does this sickness have its seat? In the power of the imagination, and possibility is its nourishment. But eternity takes away possibility. And was not this sickness oppressive enough in time—that I not only suffered but also became guilty because of it?

SLW, p. 391

If something is to be truly depressing, a presentiment must first emerge, amid all possible favorable circumstances, that, despite everything, something might nonetheless be amiss. One does not oneself become conscious of anything particularly wrong; rather, it must lie in the familial situation. Then the corrosive power of original sin manifests itself . . .

JN, vol. 2, Journal FF: 35, p. 75

Enough has been said about the light-mindedness of the age; it is high time, I think to say a little about its depression, and I hope that everything will turn out better. Or is not depression the defect of the age, is it not that which echoes even in its light-minded laughter; is it not depression that has robbed us of the courage to command, the courage to obey, the power to act, the confidence to hope?

EO,2, pp. 23–24

SELF/SPIRIT

To be spirit, that is the human being's invisible glory.

UDVS, p. 193

[N]o science can say what the self is without again stating it quite generally.

CA, p. 78

A perfect spirit cannot be conceived as sexually qualified.

CA, p. 79

Man, then, is a synthesis of psyche and body, but he is also a *synthesis of the temporal and the eternal.*

CA, p. 85

And he who is not so spiritually mature as to apprehend that even immortal honor throughout all generations is merely a qualification of the temporal, he who does not apprehend that this for which men strive and which keeps them sleepless with wishes and desire is exceedingly imperfect . . . will not get far in his explanation of spirit and immortality.

CA, pp. 102–3

Every human life is religiously designed.

CA, p. 105

There is nothing of which every man is so afraid as getting to know how enormously much he is capable of.

JP, vol. 1, no. 1007, p. 440

The phrase "know yourself" means: separate yourself from the other.

CI, p. 177

Development of spirit is self-activity; the spiritually developed individual takes his spiritual development along with him in death. If a succeeding individual is to attain it, it must occur through his self-activity; therefore he must skip nothing.

CUP, p. 345

To have been young, then to have grown older, and then finally to die is a mediocre existence, for the animal also has that merit. But to unite the elements of life in contemporaneity, that is precisely the task.

CUP, p. 348

On the battlefield, it so happens that if the first line of combatants has been victorious, then the second is not led into battle at all but merely shares in the triumph. In the world of the spirit, it is not this way.

EUD, p. 394

Just like poisonous fumes over the fields, like the hosts of grasshoppers over Egypt, so excuses and the hosts of them become a general plague that nibbles off the sprout of the eternal, become a corrupting infection among the people—with everyone who catches it there is always one more excuse available for the next person.

UDVS, p. 68

The person who lives ethically always has a way out when everything goes against him; when the darkness of the storm clouds so envelops him that his neighbor cannot see him, he still has not perished, there is always a point to which he holds fast, and that point is—himself.

EO,2, p. 253

A human being is spirit. But what is spirit? Spirit is the self. But what is the self? The self is a relation that relates itself to itself or is the relation's relating itself to itself in the relation; the self is not the relation but is the relation's relating itself to itself.

SUD, p. 13

The formula that describes the state of the self when despair is completely rooted out is this: in relating itself to itself and in willing to be itself, the self rests transparently in the power that established it.

SUD, p. 14

A person cannot rid himself of the relation to himself any more than he can rid himself of his self, which, after all, is one and the same thing, since the self is the relation to oneself.

SUD, p. 17

As a rule, a person is considered to be healthy when he himself does not say that he is sick, not to mention when he himself says that he is well. But the physician has a different view of sickness. Why? Because the physician has a defined and developed conception of what it is to be healthy and ascertains a man's condition accordingly. The physician knows that just as there is merely imaginary sickness there is also merely imaginary health . . .

SUD, p. 23

The more consciousness, the more self; the more consciousness, the more will; the more will, the more self. A person who has no will at all is not a self; but the more will he has, the more self-consciousness he has also.

SUD, p. 29

When all is said and done, whatever of feeling, knowing, and willing a person has depends upon what imagination he has, upon how that person reflects himself—that is, upon imagination.

SUD, p. 31

[F]or a self is the last thing the world cares about and the most dangerous thing of all for person to show signs of having. The greatest hazard of all, losing the self, can occur very quietly in the world, as if it were nothing at all. No other loss can occur so quietly; any other loss—an arm, a leg, five dollars, a wife, etc.—is sure to be noticed.

SUD, pp. 32–33

Despairing narrowness is to lack primitivity or to have robbed oneself of one's primitivity, to have emasculated oneself in a spiritual sense. Every human being is primitively intended to be a self, destined to become himself, and as such every self certainly is angular, but that only means that it is to be ground into shape, not that it is to be ground down smooth . . .

SUD, p. 33

When a self becomes lost in possibility in this way, it is not merely because of a lack of energy; at least it is not to be interpreted in the usual way. What is missing is essentially the power to obey, to submit to the necessity in one's life, to what may be called one's limitations.

SUD, p. 36

In order for a person to become aware of his self and of God, imagination must raise him higher than the miasma of probability, it must tear him out of this and teach him to hope and to fear—or to fear and to hope— by rendering possible that which surpasses the *quantum satis* [sufficient standard] of any experience.

SUD, p. 41

However vain and conceited men may be, they usually have a very meager conception of themselves nevertheless, that is, they have no conception of being spirit, the absolute that a human being can be; but vain and conceited they are—on the basis of comparison.

SUD, p. 43

Imagine a house with a basement, first floor, and second floor planned so that there is or is supposed to be a social distinction between the occupants according to floor. Now, if what it means to be a human being is compared with such a house, then all too regrettably the sad and ludicrous truth about the majority of people is that in their own house they prefer to live in the basement.

SUD, p. 43

There is indeed in all darkness and ignorance a dialectical interplay between knowing and willing, and in comprehending a person one may err by accentuating knowing exclusively or willing exclusively.

SUD, p. 48

The man of immediacy does not know himself, he quite literally identifies himself only by the clothes he wears, he identifies having a self by externalities (here again the infinitely comical). There is hardly a more ludicrous mistake, for a self is indeed infinitely distinct from an externality.

SUD, p. 53

When the self with a certain degree of reflection in itself wills to be responsible for the self, it may come up against some difficulty or other in the structure of the self, in the self's necessity. For just as no human body is perfect, so no self is perfect.

SUD, p. 54

There are very few persons who live even approximately within the qualification of spirit; indeed, there are not many who even try this life, and most of those who do soon back out of it. They have not learned to fear, have not learned "to have to" without any dependence, none at all, upon whatever else happens.

SUD, p. 57

The criterion for the self is always: that directly before which it is a self, but this in turn is the definition of "criterion." Just as only entities of the same kind can be added, so everything is qualitatively that by which it is measured, and that which is its qualitative criterion [*Maalestok*] is ethically its goal [*Maal*] . . .

SUD, p. 79

It is exceedingly comic that a speaker with sincere voice and gestures, deeply stirred and deeply stirring, can movingly depict the truth, can face all the powers of evil and of hell boldly, with cool self-assurance in his bearing, a dauntlessness in his air, and an appropriateness of movement worthy of admiration—it is exceedingly comic that almost simultaneously, practically still "in his dressing gown," he can timidly and cravenly cut and run away from the slightest inconvenience.

SUD, p. 91

No one is born devoid of spirit, and no matter how many go to their death with this spiritlessness as the one and only outcome of their lives, it is not the fault of life.

SUD, p. 102

Qualitatively a self is what its criterion is. That Christ is the criterion is the expression, attested by God, for the staggering reality that a self has, for only in Christ is it true that God is man's goal and criterion, or the criterion and goal.—But the more self there is, the more intense is sin.

SUD, p. 114

In every person there is something that up to a point hinders him from becoming completely transparent to himself, and this can be the case to such a high degree, he can be so inexplicably intertwined in the life—relations that lie beyond him, that he cannot open himself.

EO,2, p. 160

And this is what is sad when one contemplates human life, that so many live out their lives in quiet lostness; they outlive themselves, not in the sense that life's content successively unfolds and is now possessed in this unfolding, but they live, as it were, away from themselves and vanish like shadows. Their immortal souls are blown away, and they are not disquieted by the question of its immortality, because they are already disintegrated before they die.

EO,2, pp. 168–69

Every human being, no matter how slightly gifted he is, however subordinate his position in life may be, has a natural need to formulate a life-view, a conception of the meaning of life and of its purpose.

EO,2, p. 179

The truth of the matter is this. All of us human beings are more or less intoxicated. But we are like a drunk man who is not completely drunk so that he has lost his consciousness—no, he is definitely conscious that he is a little drunk and for that very reason is careful to conceal it from others, if possible from himself. What does he do then? He looks for something to sustain himself; he walks close to the buildings and walks erect without becoming dizzy—a sober man.

FSE, p. 113

Just as the spirit is invisible, so also is its language a secret, and the secret lies in its using the same words as the child and the simpleminded person but using them metaphorically . . .

WL, pp. 209–10

If a person does not have sufficient passion to make either of the movements, if he skulks through life repenting a little and thinking everything will come out in the wash, then he has once and for all renounced living in the idea, and in this way he can very easily achieve the highest and help others achieve it as well— that is, beguile himself and others into thinking that things happen in the world of spirit as in a game in which everything happens by chance.

FT, pp. 99–100

[T]o give in the slightest with regard to principles is to give them up, and to give up one's principles is to give up one's self.

TM, p. 319

If a man with talent is actually to become spirit, he must first of all acquire a distaste for all the satisfactions the talent has to offer—just as a lad apprenticed to the pastry trade has permission from the start to eat as many cakes and cookies as he wants—in order to acquire a distaste for cakes and cookies.

JP, vol. 4, no. 4358, p. 253

DESPAIR

Doubt is thought's despair; despair is personality's doubt.

EO,2, p. 211

But every life-view that has a condition outside itself is despair.

EO,2, p. 235

Not to be in despair is not the same as not being lame, blind, etc. If not being in despair signifies neither more nor less than not being in despair, then it means precisely to be in despair.

SUD, p. 15

When death is the greatest danger, we hope for life; but when we learn to know the even greater danger, we hope for death. When the danger is so great that death becomes the hope, then despair is the hopelessness of not even being able to die.

SUD, p. 18

If a person were to die of despair as one dies of sickness, then the eternal in him, the self, must be able to die in the same sense as the body dies of sickness. But this is impossible; the dying of despair continually converts itself into a living.

SUD, p. 18

To despair over oneself, in despair to will to be rid of oneself—this is the formula for all despair.

SUD, p. 20

[N]o human being ever lived and no one lives outside of Christendom who has not despaired and no one in Christendom if he is not a true Christian, and insofar as he is not wholly that, he still is to some extent in despair.

SUD, p. 22

As soon as man ceases to be regarded as defined by spirit (and in that case there can be no mention of despair, either) but only as psychical-physical synthesis, health is an immediate qualification, and mental or physical sickness is the only dialectical qualification. But to be unaware of being defined as spirit is precisely what despair is.

SUD, p. 25

[B]ut happiness is not a qualification of spirit, and deep, deep within the most secret hiding place of happiness there dwells also anxiety, which is despair; it very much wishes to be allowed to remain there, because for despair the most cherished and desirable place to live is in the heart of happiness.

SUD, p. 25

And when the hourglass has run out, the hourglass of temporality, when the noise of secular life has grown silent and its restless or ineffectual activism has come to an end, when everything around you is still, as it is an eternity, then—whether you were man or woman, rich or poor, dependent or independent, fortunate or unfortunate, whether you ranked with royalty and wore a glittering crown or in humble obscurity bore the toil and heat of the day, whether your name will be remembered as long as the world stands and consequently as long as it stood or you are nameless and run nameless in the innumerable multitude, whether the magnificence encompassing you surpassed all human description or the most severe and ignominious human judgment befell you—eternity asks you and every individual in these millions and millions about only one thing: whether you have lived in despair or not . . .

SUD, p. 27

[I]f you have lived in despair, then, regardless of what else you won or lost, everything is lost for you, eternity does not acknowledge you, it never knew you—or, still more terrible, it knows you as you are known and it binds you to yourself in despair.

SUD, p. 28

But if the self does not become itself, it is in despair, whether it knows that or not.

SUD, p. 30

Despair itself is a negativity; ignorance of it, a new negativity. However, to reach the truth, one must go through every negativity, for the old legend about breaking a certain magic spell is true: the piece has to be played through backwards or the spell is not broken.

SUD, p. 44

Every human existence that is not conscious of itself as spirit or conscious of itself before God as spirit, every human existence that does not rest transparently in God but vaguely rests in and merges in some abstract universality (state, nation, etc.) or, in the dark about his self, regards his capacities merely as powers to produce without becoming deeply aware of their source, regards his self, if it is to have intrinsic meaning, as an indefinable something—every such existence, whatever it achieves, be it most amazing, whatever it explains, be it the whole of existence, however intensively it enjoys life esthetically—every such existence is nevertheless despair.

SUD, p. 46

[T]he distinction must be made as to whether or not the person who is conscious of his despair has the true conception of what despair is. Admittedly, he can be quite correct, according to his own idea of despair, to say that he is in despair; he may be correct about being in despair, but that does not mean that he has the true conception of despair.

SUD, p. 47

[I]t is imperative to have clarity about oneself—that is, insofar as simultaneous clarity and despair are conceivable.

SUD, p. 47

The opposite to being in despair is to have faith.

SUD, p. 49

[H]e stands and points to what he calls despair but it is not despair, and in the meantime, sure enough, despair is right there behind him without his realizing it. It is as if someone facing away from the town hall and courthouse pointed straight ahead and said: There is the town hall and courthouse. He is correct, it is there—if he turns around.

SUD, p. 52

[T]he self in despair is satisfied with paying attention to itself, which is supposed to bestow infinite interest and significance upon his enterprises, but it is precisely this that makes them imaginary constructions.

SUD, p. 69

Most men are characterized by a dialectic of indifference and live a life so far from the good (faith) that it is almost too spiritless to be called sin—indeed, almost too spiritless to be called despair.

SUD, p. 101

Despairing as he was, he thought: What is lost is lost—yet he could not help but turn around once more in longing for the good . . .

UDVS, p. 33

But is only that person mortal who is dead, would not the person who is alive be called mortal when death is his certainty; likewise, is not that person in despair who has not even begun to despair because he has not detected that he was in despair!

UDVS, p. 278

[D]espair is the lack of the eternal.

WL, p. 41

When it is made impossible to possess the beloved in time, eternity says, "You shall love"—that is, eternity then saves love from despair by making it eternal. Suppose it is death that separates the two—then what will be of help when the survivor would sink into despair? Temporal help is an even more lamentable kind of despair; but then eternity helps. When it says, "You shall love," it is saying, "Your love has an eternal worth."

WL, p. 41

There is indeed the danger of soul: that the world will come to be empty and everything a matter of indifference to you, life without taste and nourishment, truth itself a toilsome fabrication, and death a vague thought that neither alarms nor beckons.

EUD, p. 350

It takes courage not to surrender to the shrewd or sympathetic counsel of despair that allows a person to erase himself from the number of the living; but this does not necessarily mean that every sausage peddler, fed and fattened on self-confidence, has more courage than the person who succumbed to despair.

CI, p. 327

FREEDOM

It is frightful when, right from childhood, a person's consciousness has acquired a burden that all of the soul's elasticity and all of freedom's energy cannot lift.

JN, vol. 2, Journal JJ: 71, p. 150

The entire question of the relation of God's omnipotence and God's goodness to evil can perhaps—instead of making the distinction that God accomplishes the good and merely permits what is evil—be solved quite simply in the following manner. The absolutely greatest thing that can be done for a being, greater than anything one could make it into, is to make it free. It is precisely here that omnipotence is required.

JN, vol. 4, Journal NB: 69, p. 56

[F]reedom's possibility is not the ability to choose the good or the evil. . . . The possibility is to *be able*.

CA, p. 49

How unreasonable people are! They never use the freedoms they have but demand those they do not have; they have freedom of thought—they demand freedom of speech.

EO,1, p. 19

But what is this self of mine? If I were to speak of a first moment, a first expression for it, then my answer is this: It is the most abstract of all, and yet in itself it is also the most concrete of all—it is freedom.

EO,2, p. 214

The good is because I will it, and otherwise it is not at all. This is the expression of freedom, and the same is also the case with evil—it is only inasmuch as I will it.

EO,2, p. 224

Inasmuch as the learner is in untruth but is that by his own act (and, according to what has already been said, there is no other way he can be that), he might seem to be free, for to be on one's own certainly is freedom. And yet he is indeed unfree and bound and excluded, because to be free from the truth is indeed to be excluded, and to be excluded by oneself is indeed to be bound.

PF, p. 15

[B]elief is not a knowledge but an act of freedom, an expression of will.

PF, p. 83

A pure heart. Usually we say instead that a free heart is required for love or giving oneself in love. This heart must not belong to anyone else or to anything else; yes, even the hand that gives it away must be free. It must not be the hand that takes the heart by force and gives it away, but it must rather be the heart that gives away the hand. This heart, free as it is, will then find total freedom in giving itself away.

WL, p. 147

[N]o one is as resigned as God, because he communicates creatively in such a way that in creating he *gives* independence vis-à-vis himself. The most resigned a human being can be is to acknowledge the given independence in every human being and to the best of one's ability do everything in order truly to help someone retain it.

CUP, p. 260

POSSIBILITY

The apparent abundance of thoughts and ideas that one feels in abstract possibility is just as unpleasant and elicits a similar anxiety to that which cows suffer when they are not milked on time. So when external circumstances won't help, the best thing is, as it were, to milk oneself.

JN, vol. 1, Journal DD: 28c, p. 221

Fools and young people say that everything is possible for a human being. But that is a gross error. Spiritually speaking, everything is possible, but in the finite world there is much that is not possible.

FT, p. 44

My soul has lost possibility. If I were to wish for something, I would wish not for wealth or power but for the passion of possibility, for the eye, eternally young, eternally ardent, that sees possibility everywhere. Pleasure disappoints; possibility does not.

EO,1, p. 41

When someone faints, we call for water, eau de Cologne, smelling salts; but when someone wants to despair, and the word is: Get possibility, get possibility, possibility is the only salvation. A possibility—then the person in despair breathes again, he revives again, for without possibility a person seems unable to breathe.

SUD, pp. 38–39

KIERKEGAARD AT HIS "HIGH DESK"

FIGURE 5. Kierkegaard at high desk.
Portrait by Luplau Janssen, 1902. The National Museum
of History, Frederiksborg.

The philistine–bourgeois mentality thinks that it controls possibility, that it has tricked this prodigious elasticity into the trap or madhouse of probability, thinks that it holds it prisoner; it leads possibility around imprisoned in the cage of probability . . .

SUD, pp. 41–42

CHOICE/DECISION

It is said that a golden key opens up everything. But it is certain that decisiveness and determination also open things up . . .

JN, vol. 5, NB7: 87, p. 126

The choice itself is crucial for the content of the personality: through the choice the personality submerges itself in that which is being chosen, and when it does not choose, it withers away in atrophy.

EO,2, p. 163

[T]here eventually comes a moment where it is no longer a matter of an Either/Or, not because he has chosen, but because he has refrained from it, which also can be expressed by saying: Because others have chosen for him—or because he has lost himself.

EO,2, p. 164

Already prior to one's choosing, the personality is interested in the choice, and if one puts off the choice, the personality or the obscure forces within it unconsciously chooses.

EO,2, p. 164

[W]hat is important in choosing is not so much to choose the right thing as the energy, the earnestness, and the pathos with which one chooses.

EO,2, p. 167

As soon as a person can be brought to stand at the crossroads in such a way that there is no way out for him except to choose, he will choose the right thing.

EO,2, p. 168

Rather than designating the choice between good and evil, my Either/Or designates the choice by which one chooses good and evil or rules them out. Here the question is under what qualifications one will view all existence and personally live.

EO,2, p. 169

There are many who attach great importance to having seen some extraordinary world-historical individuality face to face. They never forget this impression; it has given their souls an ideal image that ennobles their natures, and yet, however significant this very moment can be, it is nothing compared with the moment of choice.

EO,2, pp. 176–77

When around one everything has become silent, solemn as a clear, starlit night, when the soul comes to be alone in the whole world, then before one there appears, not an extraordinary human being, but the eternal power itself, then the heavens seem to open, and the *I* chooses itself or, more correctly, receives itself.

EO,2, p. 177

Choose despair, then, because the despair itself is a choice, because one can doubt [*tvivle*] without choosing it, but one cannot despair [*fortvivle*] without choosing it. And in despairing a person chooses again, and what then does he choose? He chooses himself, not in his immediacy, not as this accidental individual, but he chooses himself in his eternal validity.

EO,2, p. 211

Now he possesses himself as posited by himself—that is, as chosen by himself, as free—but in possessing himself in this way, an absolute difference becomes manifest, the difference between good and evil. As long as he has not chosen himself, this difference is latent.

EO,2, p. 223

The first condition for a resolution is to have, that is, to *will* to have a *true conception of life and of oneself.*

TDIO, p. 52

Resolution is a waking up to the eternal . . .

EUD, p. 347

Everything that becomes historical is contingent, inasmuch as precisely by coming into existence, by becoming historical, it has its element of contingency . . . therein lies again the incommensurability between a historical truth and an eternal decision.

CUP, p. 98

[T]o have been very close to making the leap is nothing whatever, precisely because the leap is the category of decision.

CUP, p. 99

What does it mean to assert that a decision is to a certain degree? It means to deny decision. Decision is designed specifically to put an end to that perpetual prattle about "to a certain degree."

CUP, p. 221

[T]he solution of doubt lies not in reflection but in resolution.

CA, p. ix

THE ETHICAL

Just as metaphysics has replaced theology, so it will finally end with physics replacing moral reflection. The whole modern statistical way of thinking of morals contributes to that.

JN, vol. 2, Journal JJ: 425, p. 260

Long ago, when people were not so calculating, one sometimes saw a noble, a magnanimous, an inspired act, genuine heroism. Now shrewdness stifles everything. If people do not manage to break free of this and learn to be quite scrupulous in scorning shrewdness (the contemptible peddler hawking earthly advantage), if they do not see that shrewdness, i.e., behaving shrewdly, corrupts oneself much more than stealing and murdering, simply because everything here is intended to lull the conscience to sleep—if they do not succeed, everything is lost.

JN, vol. 4, Journal NB2: 76, p. 171

Ethics points to ideality as a task and assumes that every man possesses the requisite conditions. Thus ethics develops a contradiction, inasmuch as it makes clear both the difficulty and the impossibility.

CA, p. 16

The more ideal ethics is, the better. It must not permit itself to be distracted by the babble that it is useless to require the impossible. For even to listen to such talk is unethical and is something for which ethics has neither *time* nor *opportunity*.

CA, p. 17

The longer life goes on and the longer the existing person through his action is woven into existence, the more difficult it is to separate the ethical from the external . . .

CUP, p. 138

In order to study the ethical, every human being is assigned to himself.

CUP, p. 141

To ask about this ethical interiority in another individual is already unethical inasmuch as it is a diversion.

CUP, p. 323

The ethical as such is the universal, and as the universal it applies to everyone, which from another angle means that it applies at all times.

FT, p. 54

If the one who is to act wants to judge himself by the result, he will never begin.

FT, p. 63

An ethics that ignores sin is a completely futile discipline, but if it affirms sin, then it has *eo ipso* exceeded itself.

FT, pp. 98–99

To desert one's post, to flee in battle, is always dishonorable, but then sagacity has come up with an ingenious turn that obligingly forestalls flight—it is evasion. Therefore, through evasion one never gets into danger and as a result does not lose one's honor by fleeing in danger.

UDVS, p. 82

And this is how perhaps the great majority of men live: they work gradually at eclipsing their ethical and ethical–religious comprehension, which would lead them out into decisions and conclusions that their lower nature does not much care for . . .

SUD, p. 94

But what does it mean to live esthetically, and what does it mean to live ethically? What is the esthetic in a person, and what is the ethical? To that I would respond: the esthetic in a person is that by which he spontaneously and immediately is what he is; the ethical is that by which he becomes what he becomes.

EO,2, p. 178

When a person has felt the intensity of duty with all his energy, then he is ethically matured, and then duty will break forth within him. The fundamental point, therefore, is not whether a person can count on his fingers how many duties he has, but that he has once and for all felt the intensity of duty in such a way that the consciousness of it is for him the assurance of the eternal validity of his being.

EO,2, p. 266

The ethical thesis that every human being has a calling expresses, then, that there is a rational order of things, in which every human being, if he so wills, fills his place in such a way that he simultaneously expresses the universally human and the individual.

EO,2, p. 292

Kant was of the opinion that man is his own law (autonomy)—that is, he binds himself under the law which he himself gives himself. Actually, in a profounder sense, this is how lawlessness or experimentation are established. This is not being rigorously earnest any more than Sancho Panza's self-administered blows to his bottom were vigorous.

JP, vol. 1, no. 188, p. 76

DECEPTION/SELF-DECEPTION

But we human beings have such a desire to live in an illusion. Alas, that is precisely why worldly greatness and renown are such a dangerous snare ... because being the object of the attention of many people ... can so easily mislead a person into drawing the erroneous conclusion that one is also more important for God.

JN, vol. 4, Journal NB: 68, p. 56

Zealousness to learn from life is seldom found, but all the more frequently a desire, inclination, and reciprocal haste to be deceived by life.

TA, p. 10

We can be deceived by believing what is untrue, but we certainly are also deceived by not believing what is true.

WL, p. 5

Which is sadder, the sight that promptly and unconditionally moves one to tears, the sight of someone unhappily deceived in love, or the sight that in a certain
sense could tempt laughter, the sight of the self-
deceived, whose fatuous conceit of not being deceived
is indeed ridiculous and laughable if the ridiculousness
of it were not an even stronger expression for horror,
since it shows that he is not worthy of tears.

WL, p. 5

Oh, there is a lot of talk in the world about treachery
and faithfulness, and, God help us, it is unfortunately
all too true, but still let us never because of this forget
that the most dangerous traitor of all is the one every
person has within himself.

WL, p. 23

When deception and truth are then placed in the
equilibrium of opposite possibilities, the decision is
whether there is mistrust or love in you. See, someone
says, "Even what appears to be the purest feeling could
still be a deception." Well, yes, that is possible; it must
be possible. "Ergo I choose mistrust or choose to believe nothing." That is, he discloses his mistrust. Let us
reverse the conclusion: "Truth and falsity reach unconditionally just as far; therefore it is possible that even
something that appears to be the vilest behavior could
be pure love." Well, yes, it is possible, it must be possible. Ergo the one who loves chooses to believe all
things—that is, he discloses his love.

WL, p. 228

But here in the world it is not "stupid" to believe ill of a good person; after all, it is an arrogance by which one gets rid of the good in a convenient way. But it is "stupid" to believe well of an evil person; so one safeguards oneself—since what one so greatly fears is being in error. On the other hand, the loving person truly fears being in error; therefore he believes all things.

WL, p. 232

If a mentally deranged person wants to convince a reasonable person of the correctness of his insane thoughts and now in a certain sense he succeeds, is this not the most appalling of all, is this not almost merciless of existence, because if he had failed, then perhaps the mentally deranged person could have become aware that he was mentally deranged, but now it is hidden from him and his mental derangement is probably incurable. The situation of the deceiver is like that . . .

WL, p. 242

The person who is deceived by the world can still hope that he will not be disappointed some other time under other circumstances, but the person who deceives himself is continually deceived even if he flees to the farthest limits of the world, because he cannot escape himself.

EUD, p. 211

It is the nature of a sickness to crave most vehemently, to love most, precisely that which is most harmful to the one who is sick. But, spiritually understood, the human being in his natural state is sick, he is in error, in a self-deception. Therefore he craves most of all to be deceived; then he is allowed not only to remain in error but to feel really at home in the self-deception.

TM, p. 225

[O]f all deceivers, fear most yourself!

TM, p. 297

Talleyrand's famous statement that man did not acquire speech in order to reveal his thoughts but in order to conceal them contains a profound irony about the world and from the angle of political prudence corresponds entirely to another genuinely diplomatic principle: *mundus vult decipi, decipiatur ergo* [the world wants to be deceived; therefore let it be deceived].

CI, pp. 253–54

GUILT

Guilt has for the eye of the spirit the fascinating power of the serpent's glance.

CA, p. 103

Whoever learns to know his guilt only by analogy to judgments of the police court and the supreme court never really understands that he is guilty, for if a man is guilty, he is infinitely guilty.

CA, p. 161

The situation of the guilty person traveling through life to eternity is like that of a murderer who fled the scene of his act—and his crime—on the express train: alas, just beneath the coach in which he sat ran the telegraph wires carrying his description and orders for his arrest at the first station.

SUD, p. 124

[T]he Omniscient One does not find out anything about the person confessing, but instead the person confessing finds out something about himself.

UDVS, p. 22

Guilt—what does it mean? Is it hexing? Is it not positively known how it comes about that a person is guilty? Will no one answer me?

R, p. 200

Ah, there are crimes that the world does not call crimes, that it rewards and almost honors—and yet, yet I would rather, God forbid, arrive in eternity with three repented murders on my conscience than as a retired slanderer . . .

WL, p. 291

In paganism the Furies were seen pursuing the guilty, their frightful figures were seen—but remorse cannot be seen, remorse is hidden, a hidden pregnancy of which a bad conscience is the father.

JN, vol. 2, Journal JJ: 334, p. 228

Human justice is very prolix, and yet at times quite mediocre; divine justice is more concise and needs no information from the prosecution . . . but makes the guilty one his own informer and helps him with eternity's memory.

EUD, p. 351

ENVY

Human envy will finally come to abolish every essential distinction, replacing it with tyrannical arbitrariness.

JN, vol. 4, Journal NB: 43, p. 43

It is a slow death to let oneself be trampled to death by geese, and to let oneself be worn to death by envy is also a slow way of dying.

JN, vol. 4, Journal NB: 209, p. 122

Envy is secret admiration. An admirer who feels that he cannot become happy by abandoning himself to it chooses to be envious of that which he admires.

SUD, p. 86

The man who told Aristides that he was voting to banish him, "because he was tired of hearing him everywhere called the only just man," actually did not deny Aristides' excellence but confessed something about himself, that his relation to this excellence was not the happy infatuation of admiration but the unhappy infatuation of envy, but he did not minimize that excellence.

TA, p. 83

Envy in the process of *establishing* itself takes the form of *leveling*, and whereas a passionate age *accelerates, raises up and overthrows, elevates and debases*, a reflective apathetic age does the opposite, it *stifles and impedes, it levels*.

TA, p. 84

THE POET

What is a poet? An unhappy person who conceals profound anguish in his heart but whose lips are so formed that as sighs and cries pass over them they sound like beautiful music. It is with him as with the poor wretches in Phalaris's bronze bull, who were slowly tortured over a slow fire; their screams could not reach the tyrant's ears to terrify him; to him they sounded like sweet music. And people crowd around the poet and say to him, "Sing again soon"—in other words, may new sufferings torture your soul, and may your lips continue to be formed as before, because your screams would only alarm us, but the music is charming.

    EO,1, p. 19

[J]ust as God created man and woman, so he created the hero and the poet or orator. The poet or orator can do nothing that the hero does; he can only admire, love, and delight in him. . . . He is recollection's genius.

    FT, p. 15

A poet is not an apostle; he drives out devils only by the power of the devil.

    FT, p. 61

Christianly understood, every poet-existence ... is sin, the sin of poetizing instead of being, of relating to the good and the true through the imagination instead of being that—that is, existentially striving to be that.

SUD, p. 77

Poetry and art have been called an anticipation of the eternal. If one wants to call them that, one must nevertheless be aware that poetry and art are not essentially related to an existing person, since the contemplation of poetry and art, "joy over the beautiful," is disinterested, and the observer is contemplatively outside himself ...

CUP, p. 313 (note)

People love the poet above all because he is to them the most dangerous of all.

TM, p. 225

This morning I saw half a score of wild geese fly away in the crisp cool air; they were right overhead at first and then farther and farther away, and at last they separated into two flocks, like two eyebrows over my eyes, which now gazed into the land of poetry.

JN, vol. 1, Journal DD: 96[a], p. 243

As the poet's song echoes with a sigh from his own unhappy love, so too will all my inspired talk about the ideal of being a Christian echo with a sigh: Alas! I am not a Christian, I am only a Christian poet and thinker.

JN, vol. 5, NB10: 200, p. 379

EROTIC LOVE

It is the most interesting time, the period of falling in love, where after the first touch of a wand's sweeping sensation, from each encounter, every glance . . . one brings something home, just like a bird busily fetching one stick after the other to her nest, yet always feels overwhelmed by the great wealth.

JN, vol. 1, Journal DD: 154, p. 255

Erotic love and marriage are really only a further confirmation of self-love—inasmuch as two unite in loving the self. It is for this very reason that married people become so satisfied and flourish with such vegetative abundance—for pure love does not conform to earthly existence the way self-love does.

JN, vol. 4, Journal NB2: 78, pp. 171–72

[I]n Christendom we have completely forgotten what love is. We pander to erotic love and friendship, honoring and praising them as love, that is, as virtues. Nonsense. Erotic love and friendship are earthly happiness, are temporal goods, just like money, gifts, talents, etc., only even better.

JN, vol. 4, Journal NB2: 83, p. 174

What does erotic love love? Infinity.—What does erotic love fear? Boundaries.

EO,1, p. 442

FIGURE 6. Regine Olsen.
Painting by Emil Baerentzen, 1840. Museum of Copenhagen.

Erotic love [*Elskov*] is still not the eternal; it is the beautiful dizziness of infinity; its highest expression is the foolhardiness of riddles.

WL, p. 19

So let the harp be tuned; let the poets' songs begin; let all be festive while erotic love [*Elskov*] celebrates its triumph, for erotic love is jubilant when it unites equal and equal and is triumphant when it makes equal in erotic love that which was unequal.

PF, p. 27

[S]pirit cannot participate in the culmination of the erotic. Let me express myself in the manner of the Greeks. The spirit is indeed present, because it is spirit that establishes the synthesis, but it cannot express itself in the erotic. It feels itself a stranger. It says, as it were, to the erotic: My dear, in this I cannot be a third party; therefore I shall hide myself for the time being.

CA, p. 71

SILENCE

Do you not believe in silence? I do. When Cain had killed Abel, Abel was silent. But Abel's blood shouts to heaven; it shouts, . . . it shouts to heaven; what terrible eloquence that never becomes silent—ah, the power of silence!

FSE, p. 46

And if I were a physician and someone asked me "What do you think should be done?" I would answer, "The first thing, the unconditional condition for anything to be done, consequently the very first thing that must be done is: create silence, bring about silence; God's Word cannot be heard, and if in order to be heard in the hullabaloo it must be shouted deafeningly with noisy instruments, then it is not God's Word; create silence!"

FSE, p. 47

Silence . . . does not consist simply in the absence of speaking. No, silence is like the subdued lighting in a pleasant room, like the friendliness in a modest living room; it is not something one talks about, but it is there and exercises its beneficent power.

FSE, p. 49

Silence is the demon's trap, and the more that is silenced, the more terrible the demon, but silence is also divinity's mutual understanding with the single individual.

FT, p. 88

Abraham remains silent—but he *cannot* speak. Therein lies the distress and anxiety. Even though I go on talking night and day without interruption, if I cannot make myself understood when I speak, then I am not speaking. This is the case with Abraham.

FT, p. 113

Surely it is speech that distinguishes humanity above the animal and then, if you like, far above the lily. But because the ability to speak is an advantage, it does not follow that the ability to be silent would not be an art or be an inferior art. On the contrary, because the human being is able to speak, the ability to be silent is an art, and a great art precisely because this advantage of his so easily tempts him.

WA, p. 10

If, however, you take time and listen more carefully, you hear—how amazing!—you hear silence, because uniformity is nevertheless also silence. In the evening, when silence rests over the land and you hear the distant bellowing from the meadow, or from the farmer's house in the distance you hear the familiar voice of the dog, you cannot say that this bellowing or this voice disturbs the silence. No, this belongs to the silence, is in a mysterious and thus in turn silent harmony with the silence; this increases it.

WA, p. 13

What is it *to chatter*? It is the annulment of the passionate disjunction between being silent and speaking. Only the person who can remain essentially silent can speak essentially, can act essentially. Silence is inwardness. Chattering gets ahead of essential speaking, and giving utterance to reflection has a weakening effect on action by getting ahead of it.

TA, p. 97

From men, man learns to speak, from the gods, to be silent.

SUD, p. 127

[S]ilence can also be an untruth . . .

PV, p. 89

[W]ithout stillness conscience does not exist at all . . .

TDIO, p. 11

And if anyone notes that darkness falls upon his soul, let him be silent, because in this condition he ought not to speak.—

TDIO, p. 137 (Supplement)

AUTHORITY

All communication of truth has become abstract: the public has become the authority, the newspapers call themselves the editorial board, the professor calls himself speculation, the priest is meditation: not one of them, not one, dares say "I."

JN, vol. 6, Journal NB11: 223, p. 133

A philosopher with authority is nonsense. For a philosopher extends no farther than his teachings extend; if I can prove that his teachings are self-contradictory, erroneous, etc., then he has nothing to say to us.

JN, vol. 6, Journal NB14: 134, p. 427

That is why people prefer being involved with ingenuity and profundity, because they can play blindman's bluff with them, but they are afraid of authority.

WL, p. 97

A king exists physically in such a way that one can physically assure oneself of it, and if it is necessary perhaps the king can very physically assure one that he exists. But God does not exist in that way. Doubt has made use of this to place God on the same level with all those who have no authority, on the same level with geniuses, poets, and thinkers . . .

WA, p. 97

Doubt and disbelief, which make faith worthless, have, among other things, also made people ashamed of obeying, of submitting to authority.

WA, p. 104

If a son were to say, "I obey my father not because he is my father but because he is a genius, or because his commands are always profound and brilliant," this filial obedience is affected. The son emphasizes something altogether wrong, emphasizes the brilliance, the profundity in a *command*, whereas a command is simply indifferent to this qualification. The son is willing to obey on the basis of the father's profundity and brilliance, and on that basis he simply cannot *obey* him, because his critical attitude with regard to whether the command is profound and brilliant undermines the obedience.

WA, p. 104

Thus all modern speculative thought is affected by having abolished *obedience* on the one hand and *authority* on the other.

WA, p. 104

GENIUS

Therefore a genius-existence is always like a fairy tale if in the deepest sense the genius does not turn inward into himself. The genius is able to do all things, and yet he is dependent upon an insignificance that no one comprehends, an insignificance upon which the genius himself by his omnipotence bestows omnipotent significance.

CA, p. 99

The genius is not like most people and would not be satisfied to be so. This is not because he disdains men, but because he is primitively concerned with himself, whereas other men and their explanations are of no help to him.

CA, p. 107

A thesis: great geniuses couldn't really read a book. While they are reading, they will always develop themselves more than understand the author.

JN, vol. 1, Journal BB: 46, p. 131

The authentic genius's appropriation of the impression of actuality is often like someone sleeping who hears the fire alarm and conveys everything into his dreaming world while the factual as such does not appear to him at all.

JN, vol. 1, Journal DD: 145, p. 253

Like a thunderstorm, genius flies against the wind.

When a boatman sails out with his skiff he usually knows the whole journey ahead of time; but when a man-of-war puts out to sea it is only after it is out on the deep that it receives its orders: thus it is with the genius; he is out on the deep and receives his orders; the rest of us know various bits and pieces about the various things we undertake.

What an age needs is not a genius—it surely has had geniuses enough—but a martyr, one who in order to teach people to obey would himself become obedient to the point of death, one whom men put to death; but, see, just because of that they would lose, for simply by killing him, by being victorious in this way, they would become afraid of themselves. This is the awakening that our age needs.

There are two types of geniuses. Thunder is characteristic of the first type; lightning, on the other hand, is rare and seldom strikes. The second type contains within itself a category of reflection with which it disciplines itself or restrains the thunder. But then the lightning is all the more intense; it strikes the chosen points with lightning's swiftness and certainty—and deadliness.

WRITING/COMMUNICATION

Writing is not speaking; sitting at a desk and copying what is said is only baneful toil in comparison with stepping forth in an assembly, looking at a great throng who all are inspired by the same thing and for the same thing, having the stillness enter in like the prayer before battle, having the word break forth like the thunder of combat, being oneself transported by the silence that is the silence of attention, hearing the whisper that is the whisper of approval, sensing the stentoriousness of the Amen of conviction.

P, p. 27

To write a book is the easiest of all things in our time, if, as is customary, one takes ten older works on the same subject and out of them puts together an eleventh on the same subject.

P, p. 35

An expert judge in this matter has said that one rarely sees anyone who writes humbly about humility, doubtingly about doubt, etc. In other words, one rarely finds an exposition of which it holds true that the exposition is that which is expounded . . .

FSE, p. 119

I do not know to whom I am speaking about this, whether anyone is concerned about such things; but this I know, that such people have lived, and this I know, that the very people who have praised love effectually have been experienced sailors and able seamen in these waters that nowadays are in part almost unknown. And for them I can write, comforting myself with the beautiful words: "Write!" "For whom?" "For the dead, for those whom you have loved in some past."

WL, p. 362

But all true helping begins with a humbling. The helper must first humble himself under the person he wants to help and thereby understand that to help is not to dominate but to serve . . .

PV, p. 45

To be a teacher is not to say: This is the way it is, nor is it to assign lessons and the like. No, to be a teacher is truly to be the learner. Instruction begins with this, that you, the teacher, learn from the learner, place yourself in what he has understood and how he has understood it . . .

PV, p. 46

An author's work should bear the imprint of his likeness, his individuality, in the same way as the portrait that Christ is said to have sent to King Abgarus of Edessa; it was not a minutely detailed reproduction but, in some inexplicably miraculous way, a sort of emanation onto the canvas.

JN, vol. 1, Journals DD: 151, p. 255

But there must be something that is so blessed that it cannot be expressed in words. Otherwise, why were the men to whom something truly great was revealed struck dumb?—

JN, vol. 1, Journal FF: 33, p. 75

There are remarks and feelings that are expressed in the sort of medium in which they only become visible when they are fired by the warmth of sympathy and the flames of enthusiasm—as with the sort of paper on which writing only becomes visible when it is held up to the light.—

JN, vol. 2, Journal FF: 57, p. 80

This is indeed the profound untruth about all modern lectures: there is absolutely no notion of how the idea is affected when the person who presents it doesn't dare express it in actions; precisely for this reason the heart and soul of the idea disappear; the power of the idea is eliminated.

JN, vol. 4, Journal NB4: 72, p. 322

Following the path of the commentators is often like traveling to London; true, the road leads to London, but if one wants to get there, he has to turn around.

JP, vol. 1, no. 203, p. 83

All human speech, even divine speech of Holy Scripture, about the spiritual is essentially metaphorical speech.

WL, p. 209

THE PRESS

The press is really that which annihilates all personality; that a cowardly wretch can sit in concealment and write and publish for thousands. All personal conduct and all personal power must come to naught on this.

JN, vol. 4, Journal NB: 20, p. 28

Figure 7. *The Corsair.*
From *The Corsair*, Issue 285, March 6, 1846.

With the help of the degeneracy of the press, human beings will at last be made into complete idiots. A journal's first concern has to be circulation; from then on, the rule for what it publishes can be this: the cleverness and hilarity of printing something that has nothing to do with communicating in print.

JN, vol. 4, Journal NB2: 25, p. 148

The daily press is and will remain the evil principle in the modern world. There is no limit to its sophistry, because it can sink ever lower in its choice of readers. In consequence, it dredges up so much muck that no state is capable, any longer, of restraining it.

JN, vol. 4, Journal NB2: 29, p. 150

In the most ancient of times, judges and prophets watched over a country's ethos. Later it was traditional for the clergy to do it.

Then, because of worldliness, the church doubted—and the "newspapers"—and the public became ethical authorities! Finally, the most degraded part of the daily press, under the name of satire, kept a watch over ethics! [T]his is something like sending a young girl to a brothel—to safeguard her innocence.

JN, vol. 6, Journal NB11: 44, pp. 27–28

In fact, if the daily press, like some other occupational groups, had a coat-of-arms, the inscription ought to be: Here men are demoralized in the shortest possible time, on the largest possible scale, at the cheapest possible price.

JP, vol. 2, no. 2171, p. 489

In contrast to the age of revolution, which took action, the present age is an age of publicity, the age of miscellaneous announcements: nothing happens but still there is instant publicity.

TA, p. 70

In a certain sense there is something horrible about contemplating the whole mob of publishers, booksellers, journalists, authors—all of them working day and night in the service of confusion, because men will not become sober and understand that relatively little knowledge is needed to be truly human—but all the more self-knowledge.

JP, vol. 1, no. 649, p. 269

Evaluation by newspapers will gradually be extended to cover subjects never dreamed of.

JP, vol. 2, no. 2145, p. 478

SCIENCE

Here it might well seem that there is a difficulty, inasmuch as natural science, the eagerness to understand, has made its votaries and adherents enthusiastic, and thus to this extent understanding and enthusiasm do not appear to conflict with one another. It must, however, be noted that a speculative thinker, e.g., a natural scientist, etc., who is really and truly enthusiastic in grasping and understanding things, does not notice that he himself is continually positing that which he wants to abrogate. He is enthusiastic about understanding everything else, but he does not come to understand that he himself is enthusiastic—that is, he does not come to conceptualize his own enthusiasm even though, in this enthusiasm, he is enthusiastic about conceptualizing everything else.

JN, vol. 4, Journal NB: 70, p. 58, lines 26–37

In our times, it is especially the natural sciences that are dangerous. Physiology will ultimately expand so much that it will annex ethics. Indeed, there are already signs of a new attempt to treat ethics as physics, whereby the whole of ethics becomes an illusion, and the ethical aspect of the human race will be treated statistically . . .

JN, vol. 4, Journal NB: 70, p. 59, lines 3–9

When a man makes the statement, both simple and profound, that "I cannot see with my naked eye how consciousness comes into being," this is perfectly proper. But when a man has a microscope in front of his eye and looks and looks and looks—and yet cannot see it, this is comical.

JN, vol. 4, Journal NB: 73, p. 62, lines 27–31

Then we are informed by sophistical physiology that "the key to the knowledge of the conscious mental life lies in the unconscious" (Carus). But if one cannot explain the transition from unconsciousness to consciousness, what does this say about the key[?]

JN, vol. 4, Journal NB: 73, p. 64, lines 38–41

Absolutely no benefit can be derived from involving oneself with the natural sciences. One stands there defenseless, with no control over anything. The researcher immediately begins to distract one with his details: Now one is to go to Australia; now to the moon; now into an underground cave; now, by Satan, up the ass—to look for an intestinal worm; now the telescope must be used; now the microscope: Who the Devil can endure it!

JN, vol. 4, Journal NB: 87, pp. 71–72

PHILOSOPHY

Philosophy is life's dry nurse, it can look after us but not give suck.

JN, vol. 1, Journal AA: 47, p. 45

With every step it takes, philosophy sheds a skin and into it creep the more foolish adherents.

JN, vol. 1, Journal BB: 36, p. 116

In the realm of thought there is a haggling, an up-to-a-certain-point understanding, which leads to nonsense just as surely as good intentions lead to hell.

JN, vol. 2, Journal JJ: 204, p. 189

That God could create beings who are free in relation to himself is the cross that philosophy could not bear but upon which it has remained hanging.

JN, vol. 2, Journal FF: 149, p. 95

It is quite true what philosophy says, that life must be understood backward. But then one forgets the other principle, that it must be *lived forward*. Which principle, the more one thinks it through, ends exactly with temporal life never being able to be properly understood . . .

JN, vol. 2, Journal JJ: 167, p. 179

Philosophy's idea is mediation—Christianity's is the paradox.

JN, vol. 3, Notebook 7: 22, p. 207

Kant's theory of radical evil has only one flaw, that he does not firmly determine that the inexplicable is a category, that the paradox is a category. Everything turns on this. For people have continually said this sort of thing: that to say that one cannot understand something or other does not satisfy scholarly science, which wishes to grasp things conceptually. This is the seat of the error; one must say precisely the opposite: that if *human* scholarly science will not acknowledge that there is something it cannot understand—or, to be even more exact, something concerning which it clearly understands that it cannot understand—then everything is confused.

JN, vol. 4, Journal NB: 125, p. 88

In the old days they loved wisdom . . . nowadays they love the title of philosopher.

JN, vol. 4, Journal NB5: 144, p. 428

The stone which was laid before Christ's grave could well be called *the philosophers' stone*, it seems to me, inasmuch as its removal has given not only the Pharisees but now for 1,800 years the philosophers a good deal to do.

JP, vol. 3, no. 3243, p. 496

In the earlier ancient period the philosopher was a power, an ethical power, a [person of] character—then the empire protected itself by putting them on salary, by making them "professors."

JP, vol. 3, no. 3316, p. 521

Philosophy cannot and must not give faith, but it must understand itself and know what it offers and take nothing away, least of all trick men out of something by pretending that it is nothing.

FT, p. 33

What philosophers say about actuality [*Virkelighed*] is often just as disappointing as it is when one reads on a sign in a secondhand shop: Pressing Done Here. If a person were to bring his clothes to be pressed, he would be duped, for the sign is merely for sale.

EO,1, p. 32

Of what use was it to find out that there is an eternal philosophy that everyone should embrace if everyone did not learn how to go about doing it or if no one at all learned it, if at least none of the listeners had learned more than he? And yet it pained him; he thought the words to be so beautiful that he could not stop listening to them, just as one sadly gazes after the wild geese flying in the sky. Anyone who wants to belong to that world must join them, and yet no one has ever been seen flying with them.

JC, p.148

FIGURE 8. Grib Forest.
Print by S. H. Petersen, 1820. From the original in the
Museum of Coppenhagen. Reproduced by permission
of the Museum of Copenhagen.

EXISTENCE

[W]hat is existence? It is that child who is begotten by the infinite and the finite, the eternal and the temporal, and is therefore continually striving,

CUP, p. 92

Existence itself, existing, is a striving and is just as pathos-filled as it is comic: pathos-filled because the striving is infinite, that is, directed toward the infinite, is a process of infinitizing, which is the highest pathos; comic because the striving is a self-contradiction.

CUP, p. 92

A system of existence [*Tilværelsens System*] cannot be given.

CUP, p. 118

Abstractly viewed, system and existence cannot be thought conjointly, because in order to think existence, systematic thought must think it as annulled and consequently not as existing. Existence is the spacing that holds apart; the systematic is the conclusiveness that combines.

CUP, p. 118

[I]t is the misfortune of our age that it has come to know too much, has forgotten what it means to exist . . .

CUP, p. 269

Just as existence has joined thinking and existing, inasmuch as an existing person is a thinking person, so are there two media: the medium of abstraction and the medium of actuality.

CUP, p. 314

For the existing person, existing is for him his highest interest, and his interestedness in existing is his actuality. What actuality is cannot be rendered in the language of abstraction.

CUP, p. 314

All knowledge about actuality is possibility. The only actuality concerning which an existing person has more than knowledge about is his own actuality, that he exists, and this actuality is his absolute interest.

CUP, p. 316

Existence is always the particular; the abstract does not *exist*.

CUP, p. 330

The subjective thinker is not a scientist-scholar; he is an artist. To exist is an art.

CUP, p. 351

The spheres are related as follows: immediacy, finite common sense; irony, ethics with irony as its incognito; humor; religiousness with humor as its incognito—and then, finally, the essentially Christian, distinguished by the paradoxical accentuation of existence, by the paradox, by the break with immanence, and by the absurd.

CUP, pp. 531–32n

Precisely by coming into existence, everything that comes into existence demonstrates that it is not necessary, for the only thing that cannot come into existence is the necessary, because the necessary *is*.

PF, p. 74

THE ABSURD

What, then, is the absurd? The absurd is that the eternal truth has come into existence in time, that God has come into existence, has been born, has grown up, etc., has come into existence exactly as an individual human being, indistinguishable from any other human being . . .

CUP, p. 210

This concept of improbability, the absurd, ought then to be developed, for it is nothing but superficiality to think that the absurd is not a concept, that all sorts of absurdities belong equally under the absurd. No, the concept of the absurd is precisely to grasp the fact that it cannot and must not be grasped.

CUP (Vol. 2, Supplement), pp. 98–99

The *absurd*, the *paradox*, is composed in such a way that reason has no power at all to dissolve it in nonsense and prove that it is nonsense; no, it is a symbol, a riddle, a compounded riddle about which reason must say: I cannot solve it, it cannot be understood, but it does not follow thereby that it is nonsense.

CUP (Vol. 2, Supplement), p. 99

It is evident that sorrow can make a man mentally ill, and that is hard enough; it is also evident that there is a willpower that can haul to the wind so drastically that it rescues the understanding, even though a person becomes a little odd (and I do not intend to disparage this). But to be able to lose one's understanding and along with it everything finite, for which it is the stockbroker, and then to win the very same finitude again by virtue of the absurd—this appalls me, but that does not make me say it is something inferior, since, on the contrary, it is the one and only marvel.

FT, p. 36

The absurd does not belong to the differences that lie within the proper domain of the understanding. It is not identical with the improbable, the unexpected, the unforeseen.

FT, p. 46

And what higher movement has the age discovered, now that entering the monastery has been abandoned? Is it not a wretched worldly wisdom, sagacity, pusillanimity, that sits in the place of honor, that cravenly deludes men into thinking that they have performed the highest and slyly keeps them from even attempting the lesser? The person who has made the monastic movement has only one movement left, the movement of the absurd. How many in our day understand what the absurd is?

FT, p. 101

PARADOX

The paradox is the authentic *pathos* of the intellectual life, and just as only great souls are susceptible to passions, so are only great thinkers susceptible to what I call paradoxes, which are nothing other than grandiose thoughts, not yet fully developed.

JN, vol. 2, Journal FF: 152, p. 95

But one must not think ill of the paradox, for the paradox is the passion of thought, and the thinker without the paradox is like the lover without passion: a mediocre fellow.

PF, p. 37

But the ultimate potentiation of every passion is always to will its own downfall, and so it is also the ultimate passion of the understanding [*Forstand*] to will the collision, although in one way or another the collision must become its downfall. This, then, is the ultimate paradox of thought: to want to discover something that thought itself cannot think.

PF, p. 37

If the paradox and the understanding meet in the mutual understanding of their difference, then the encounter is a happy one, like erotic love's understanding—happy in the passion to which we as yet have given no name and which we shall not name until later. If the encounter is not in mutual understanding, then the relation is unhappy, and the understanding's unhappy love, if I dare call it that (which, please note, resembles only the unhappy love rooted in misunderstood self-love; since the power of chance is capable of nothing here, the analogy stretches no further), we could more specifically term *offense*.

PF, p. 49

But then is faith just as paradoxical as the paradox? Quite so. How else could it have its object in the paradox and be happy in its relation to it? Faith itself is a wonder, and everything that is true of the paradox is also true of faith.

PF, p. 65

The eternal truth has come into existence in time. That is the paradox.

CUP, p. 209

The paradox of faith, then, is this: that the single individual is higher than the universal, that the single individual . . . determines his relation to the universal by his relation to the absolute, not his relation to the absolute by his relation to the universal.

FT, p. 70

THE UNDERSTANDING/REASON/KNOWLEDGE

There is an old saying that to understand and to understand are two things, and so they are. . . . To understand a speech is one thing, and to understand what it refers to, namely, the personal, is something else; . . .

CA, p. 142

In every generation, most people . . . live and die in the delusion that things keep on going, and that if it were granted them to live longer, things would keep going onward in a continuing, straightforward ascent with more and more comprehension. How many experience at all the maturity of discovering that there comes a critical point where things turn around, when what matters from then on is an increasing comprehension that more and more comprehends that there is something that cannot be comprehended[?]

JN, vol. 6, Journal NB12: 134, p. 225

FIGURE 9. Kierkegaard as student.
Portrait by David Jacob Jacobsen, 1840. The Museum
of National History, Frederiksborg.

To sit in a room where everything is so quiet that one
can hear a grain of sand fall and can understand the
highest—that every person can do. But, to speak figuratively, to sit in the kettle the coppersmith is ham-
mering on and then to understand the same thing—

well, then one must have the understanding close at hand . . .

WL, pp. 78–79

The understanding counts and counts, calculates and calculates, but it never arrives at the certainty that faith possesses . . .

WL, p. 105

So also with knowing when it becomes fantastic. The law for the development of the self with respect to knowing, insofar as it is the case that the self becomes itself, is that the increase of knowledge corresponds to the increase of self-knowledge, that the more the self knows, the more it knows itself.

SUD, p. 31

Does this mean, then, that to understand and to understand are two different things? They certainly are, and the person who has understood this—but, please note, not in the sense of the first kind of understanding—is *eo ipso* initiated into all the secrets of irony.

SUD, p. 90

What, then, is the unknown? It is the frontier that is continually arrived at, and therefore when the category of motion is replaced by the category of rest it is the different, the absolutely different. But it is the absolutely different in which there is no distinguishing mark.

PF, pp. 44–45

Honor be to learning and knowledge; praised be the one who masters the material with the certainty of knowledge, with the reliability of autopsy.

CUP, p. 11

All my work oriented to knowing does not touch my life at all, its desires, its passions, its selfishness, and leaves me completely unchanged—my action changes my life.

FSE, p. 116

This is the truth of the matter. In every human being there is a capacity, the capacity for knowledge. And every person—the most knowing and the most limited—is in his knowing far beyond what he is in his life or what his life expresses.

FSE, p. 118

But one thing is sure, reflection, like knowledge, increases sorrow, and beyond a doubt there is no task and effort more difficult for the individual as well as for the whole generation than to extricate oneself from the temptations of reflection . . .

TA, p. 77

[W]hen the understanding stands still, it behooves one to have the courage and the heart to believe the wondrous and, continually strengthened by this vision, to return to actuality and not just sit still and want to fathom it.

SLW, p. 122

TRUTH

Truth has always had many loud proclaimers, but the question is whether a person will in the deepest sense acknowledge the truth, will allow it to permeate his whole being, will accept all its consequences, and not have an emergency hiding place for himself and a Judas kiss for the consequence.

CA, p. 138

There is one view of life that holds that wherever the multitude is, there, too, is the truth—that truth itself needs to have the multitude on its side. There is another view of life that holds that wherever the multitude is, there is untruth, so that even if every individual, silently and separately, possessed the truth, nonetheless if they assembled in a multitude (in such a way that *the multitude* had any sort of decisive, electoral, noisy, audible significance), then untruth would immediately be present.

JN, vol. 4, Journal NB: 56, p. 54

How many an individual has not asked, "What is truth?" and at bottom hoped that it would be a long time before the truth would come so close to him that in the same instant it would determine what it was his duty to do at that moment.

WL, p. 96

FIGURE 10. Kierkegaard grave.
Photograph by Wayne Wakeman, 2002.

Let us take the knowledge of God as an example. Objectively, what is reflected upon is that this is the true God; subjectively, that the individual relates himself to a something *in such a way* that his relation is in truth a God-relation. Now, on which side is the truth?

CUP, p. 199

The *how* of the truth is precisely the truth.
   CUP, p. 323

[F]or only the truth that builds up is truth for you.
   EO,2, p. 354

TIME

Thus understood, the moment is not properly an atom of time but an atom of eternity. It is the first reflection of eternity in time, its first attempt, as it were, at stopping time.

CA, p. 88

Nature's security has its source in the fact that time has no significance at all for nature. Only with the moment does history begin.

CA, p. 89

If there is no next day for you, then either you are dying or you are one who by dying to temporality grasped the eternal, either one who is actually dying or one who is *really* living.

CD, p. 72

If it is true that time changes everything, the changeable, then it is also true that time reveals who it was who did not change.

TA, p. 7

All the forces of life are incapable of resisting time; it sweeps them along with itself—even recollection is in the present.

TDIO, p. 78

Indeed, time [*Tid*] also is a good. If a person were able to produce a scarcity [*Dyrtid*] in the external world, yes, then he would be busy.

TDIO, p. 83

Who has not heard how one day, sometimes one hour, gained infinite worth because death made time dear! Death is able to do this, but with the thought of death the earnest person is able to create a scarcity so that the year and the day receive infinite worth . . .

TDIO, p. 84

What is joy, or what is it to be joyful? It is truly to be present to oneself; but truly to be present to oneself is this *today*, this *to be* today, truly *to be today*. The more true it is that you are today, the more completely present you are to yourself today, the less the day of trouble, tomorrow, exists for you. Joy is the present time with the whole emphasis on: *the present time*.

WA, p. 39

Time, or the fact that suffering drags on in time, is always the most oppressive suffering. Daily worries, daily derision year in and year out, are far worse than any catastrophe, because, among other things, this always looks like nothing to an outside observer.

JN, vol. 4, Journal NB2: 80, p. 172

In relation to the absolute, there is only one time, the present; for the person who is not contemporary with the absolute, it does not exist at all.

PC, p. 63

Alas, why did time come into existence! If the good has always been victorious eternally, why must it drag itself slowly forward through the duration of time or almost perish in the slowness of time, why must it struggle laboriously through what makes time so long, through uncertainty!

UDVS, p. 61

Alas, time comes and time goes, it subtracts little by little; then it deprives a person of a good, the loss of which he indeed feels, and his pain is great. Alas, and he does not discover that long ago it has already taken away from him the most important thing of all—the capacity to make a resolution . . .

TDIO, p. 48

ETERNAL

Many people are afraid of eternity—if only we can endure time, we can surely deal with eternity. Thus when one hears lovers vow to love one another for eternity, it does not mean nearly as much as when they promise to do so in time, because the person who makes such a promise for eternity can always answer that for the time being you'll have to excuse me.

JN, vol. 3, Notebook 7: 38, pp. 210–11

[D]enial of the eternal may express itself directly or indirectly in many various ways, as mockery, as prosaic intoxication with common sense, as busyness, as enthusiasm for the temporal, etc.

CA, p. 152

Some bend eternity into time for the imagination. Conceived in this way, eternity produces an enchanting effect. One does not know whether it is dream or actuality. As the beams of the moon glimmer in an illuminated forest or a hall, so the eternal peeps wistfully, dreamily, and roguishly into the moment. Thought of the eternal becomes a fanciful pottering around, and the mood is always the same: Am I dreaming, or is it eternity that is dreaming of me?

CA, p. 152

Resolution is a waking up to the eternal . . .

EUD, p. 347

Alas, time and busyness think that eternity is very far away . . .

UDVS, p. 66

Wherever the eternal is, there is rest; but there is unrest where the eternal is not present.

UDVS, p. 258

For an existing person, the goal of motion is decision and repetition. The eternal is the continuity of motion, but an abstract eternity is outside motion, and a concrete eternity in the existing person is the maximum of passion.

CUP, p. 312

Only the eternal can be and become and remain contemporary with every age . . .

WL, p. 31

Thus the one who actually occupies himself with the eternal is never busy.

WL, p. 98

DEATH

But even if it is very pleasant for flesh and blood to avoid opposition, I wonder if it is a comfort also in the hour of death. In the hour of death, surely the only comfort is that one has not avoided opposition but has suffered it.

WL, p. 84

It is a task, and one need not have seen much in life to have seen enough to be assured that it may very well be necessary to emphasize that it is a task, a duty, to recollect the dead. The untrustworthiness of human feelings left to their own devices perhaps never manifests itself more than in this very relationship.

WL, p. 348

Parents love the children almost before they come into existence and long before they become conscious beings, therefore as nonbeings. But a dead person is also a nonbeing, and the two greatest good works are these: to give a human being life and to recollect one who is dead; yet the first work of love has a repayment.

WL, p. 349

There are, as is known, insects that die in the moment of fertilization. So it is with all joy: life's highest, most splendid moment of enjoyment is accompanied by death.

EO,1, p. 20

In the grave there is no recollection, not even of God. See, the man did know this, the one of whom it must now be said that he no longer recollects anything, to whom it would now be too late to say this.

TDIO, p. 71

Death can expressly teach that earnestness lies in the inner being, in thought, can teach that it is only an illusion when the external is regarded light-mindedly or heavy-mindedly or when the observer, profoundly considering the thought of death, forgets to think about and take into account his own death.

TDIO, p. 73

To think of oneself as dead is earnestness; to be a witness to the death of another is mood.

TDIO, p. 75

When death comes, the word is: Up to here, not one step further, then it is concluded, not a letter is added; the meaning is at an end and not one more sound is to be heard—all is over.

TDIO, pp. 78–79

Death in earnest gives life force as nothing else does; it makes one alert as nothing else does.

TDIO, p. 83

When sickness becomes a daily visitor and time passes, the time of joy, and even those closest become weary of the suffering one and many an impatient word wounds, when the sufferer himself feels that his mere presence is disturbing to the joyful, and so you must sit far away from the dance—then it is supposed to be a relief to reflect that death invites him also to the dance, and in that dance all become equal.

TDIO, p. 87

So death is indefinable—the only certainty, and the only thing about which nothing is certain.

TDIO, p. 91

What is decisive about the explanation, what prevents the nothingness of death from annihilating the explanation, is that it acquires retroactive power and actuality in the life of the living person; then death becomes a teacher to him and does not traitorously assist him to a confession that denounces the explainer as a fool.

TDIO, p. 97

And this testing by death—or with a more commonly used foreign word to designate the same thing—this final examination [*Examen*] of life, is equally difficult for all. It is not as it usually is—namely, that the fortunately gifted person passes easily and the poorly gifted person has a hard time—no, death adapts the test to the ability—oh, so very accurately, and the test becomes equally difficult because it is the test of earnestness.

TDIO, p. 102

[J]ust as nature declares God, so every grave preaches.

TDIO, p. 109

Move on, you drama of life—let no one call it a comedy, no one a tragedy, for no one saw the end! Move on, you drama of existence, where life is not given again any more than money is! Why has no one returned from the dead? Because life does not know how to captivate as death does, because life does not have the persuasiveness that death has.

R, p. 176

"Just as the captive beast walks round in the cage every day for the sake of exercise, or measures the length of the chain, so I too measure the length of the chain every day by walking to the thought of death—for the sake of exercise and to put up with living."

JN, vol. 4, Journal NB3: 7, p. 248

IMMORTALITY

A book propounds the question of the immortality of the soul; the contents of the book are, of course, the answer. But the contents of the book, as the reader convinces himself by reading it through, consist of all the wisest and best men's opinions, strung on a thread, concerning immortality. . . . But essentially the question of immortality is not a learned question; it is a question belonging to inwardness, which the subject by becoming subjective must ask himself.

CUP, p. 173

It [demonstrating immortality] is like wanting to paint Mars in the armor that makes him invisible.

CUP, p. 174

Immortality is judgment. There is not one more word to say about immortality; the one who says one more word or a word in another direction had better beware of judgment.

CD, p. 206

Immortality could not be a final change that intervened . . . it is a changelessness that is not changed with
the change of the years.

UDVS, pp. 10–11

The distant baying of a dog, calling one to far-off,
friendly, familiar places—constitutes the most beautiful proof of the immortality of the soul.

JN, vol. 2, Journal FF: 71, p. 83

REPETITION

Repetition and recollection are the same movement,
except in opposite directions, for what is recollected
has been, is repeated backward, whereas genuine repetition is recollected forward.

R, p. 131

He alone is truly happy who is not deluded into thinking that the repetition should be something new, for
then one grows weary of it.

R, p. 132

Repetition is the new category that will be discovered. . . . The dialectic of repetition is easy, for that
which is repeated has been—otherwise it could not be

repeated—but the very fact that it has been makes repetition into something new.

R, pp. 148–49

If one does not have the category of recollection or repetition, all life dissolves into an empty, meaningless noise. Recollection is the ethnical [*ethniske*] view of life, repetition the modern; repetition is the *interest* [*Interesse*] of metaphysics, and also the interest upon which metaphysics comes to grief; repetition is the watchword [*Løsnet*] in every ethical view; repetition is *conditio sine qua non* [the indispensable condition] for every issue of dogmatics.

R, p. 149

When ideality and reality touch each other, then repetition occurs.

JC, p. 171

BUSYNESS

There [is] no one I would rather have fall down, or have Knippelbro raised in front of, etc. than these hard pressed businessmen who have so infinitely much to get done in the world, while the rest of us, when Knippelbro is raised, find it a good opportunity to fall into a reverie—

JN, vol. 3, Notebook 5: 6, p. 172

FIGURE 11. Kierkegaard in the street.
By Luplau Janssen, 1902. Photo by Lennart Larsen.
The National Museum of History, Frederiksborg.

The result of busyness is that an individual is very seldom permitted to form a heart.

JN, vol. 4, Journal NB: 92, p. 74

This is the situation: in the eternal sense there is absolutely nothing to hurry after, and nonetheless ... I must be as diligent as the most diligent, as frugal with time as a beggar is with a shilling, and I must occupy myself most carefully and calmly with every little detail.

JN, vol. 4, Journal NB: 214, p. 124

To be busy is to occupy oneself, divided and scattered (which follows from the object that occupies one), with all the multiplicity in which it is simply impossible for a person to be whole, whole in all of it or whole in any particular part of it, something only the insane can succeed in doing.

WL, p. 98

A mirror, it is true, has the feature that a person can see his image in it, but then one must stand still. If one hastily hurries by, one gets to see nothing.

UDVS, p. 67

THE INDIVIDUAL

There is at once something very humbling and yet infinitely elevating for the individual in the fact that God concerns himself just as much, absolutely just as much, with the least [human being] as with the greatest.

JN, vol. 4, Journal NB: 68, p. 56

To will to be an individual human being (which one unquestionably is) with the help of and by virtue of one's difference is flabbiness; but to will to be an individual existing human being (which one unquestionably is) in the same sense as everyone else is capable of being—that is the ethical victory over life and over every mirage . . .

CUP, p. 356

Everyone must make an accounting to God as an individual; the king must make an accounting to God as an individual, and the most wretched beggar must make an accounting to God as an individual—lest anyone be arrogant by being more than an individual, lest anyone despondently think that he is not an individual . . .

UDVS, p. 128

Eternity does not ask whether you brought up your children the way you saw others doing it but asks you as an individual how you brought up your children.

UDVS, pp. 130–31

[I]f I have spoken erroneously, and insofar as I have spoken erroneously, I will be asked about it as a single individual and without any excuses. In eternity there is not the remotest thought of any collective failure. In eternity the single individual, you, my listener, and I, will be questioned as the single individual, alone by himself as an individual . . .

UDVS, p. 149

LAUGHTER/HUMOR/THE COMIC

[T]he comical always consists in *contradiction*. If a man seeks permission to establish himself as a proprietor of an alehouse and is refused, it is not comical. On the other hand, if a girl seeks permission to establish herself as a prostitute and is refused, which sometimes happens, then it is comical . . .

JN, vol. 2, Journal JJ: 276, pp. 208–9

Humor can be either religious or demonic (in relation to the two mysteries)[.]

JN, vol. 3, Notebook 5: 30, p. 183

One must see how no attack is so feared as that of laughter, how even the person who courageously risked his life for a stranger would not be far from betraying his father and mother if the danger was laughter, because more than any other this attack isolates the one attacked . . .

PV, p. 65

Something marvelous has happened to me. I was transported to the seventh heaven. There sat all the gods assembled. As a special dispensation, I was granted the favor of making a wish. "What do you want," asked Mercury. "Do you want youth, or beauty, or power, or a long life, or the most beautiful girl, or anyone of the other glorious things we have in the treasure chest? Choose—but only one thing." For a moment I was bewildered; then I addressed the gods, saying: My esteemed contemporaries, I choose one thing—that I may always have the laughter on my side. Not one of the gods said a word; instead, all of them began to laugh. From that I concluded that my wish was granted and decided that the gods knew how to express themselves with good taste, for it would indeed have been inappropriate to reply solemnly: It is granted to you.

    EO,1, pp. 42–43

The comic is always a sign of maturity ... I consider the power in the comic a vitally necessary legitimation for anyone who is to be regarded as authorized in the world of spirit in our day. . . . But assistant professors are so devoid of comic power that it is shocking ...

    CUP, p. 281

To aspire to wittiness without possessing the wealth of inwardness is like wanting to be prodigal on luxuries and to dispense with the necessities of life ...

    TA, p. 74

The more one suffers, the more sense, I believe, one gains for the comic. Only by the most profound suffering does one gain real competence in the comic, which with a word magically transforms the rational creature called man into a *Fratze* [caricature].

SLW, p. 245

THE TRAGIC

[N]o matter how much the world has changed, the idea of the tragic is still essentially unchanged, just as weeping still continues to be equally natural to humankind.

EO,1, p. 139

The tragic and the comic are the same inasmuch as both are contradiction, but *the tragic is suffering contradiction, and the comic is painless contradiction.*

CUP, p. 514

I too have combined the tragic with the comic: I make witticisms, people laugh—I cry.

JN, vol. 1, Journal DD: 33, p. 225

Doubtless the most sublime tragedy consists in being *misunderstood.* For this reason the life of Christ is supreme tragedy.

JP, vol. 1, no. 118, p. 50

IRONY

Irony is an abnormal development which, like the abnormality in the livers of Strasbourg geese, ends by killing the individual.

JN, vol. 2, Journal FF: 159, p. 97

Irony is the unity of ethical passion, which in inwardness ethically accentuates one's own I, and cultivation, which in outwardness (in associating with human beings) infinitely abstracts from one's own I.

JN, vol. 2, Journal JJ: 323, p. 223

But just as there is something deterring about irony, it likewise has something extraordinarily seductive and fascinating. Its masquerading and mysteriousness, the telegraphic communication it prompts because an ironist always has to be understood at a distance . . .

CI, p. 48

The ironist is the vampire who has sucked the blood of the lover and while doing so has fanned him cool, lulled him to sleep, and tormented him with troubled dreams.

CI, p. 49

The ironic figure of speech has still another property that characterizes all irony, a certain superiority deriving from its not wanting to be understood immedi-

FIGURE 12. Hansen drawing of Kierkegaard.
Drawing by H. P. Hansen, 1854. Royal Library, Copenhagen.

ately, even though it wants to be understood, with the result that this figure looks down, as it were, on plain and simple talk that everyone can promptly understand . . .

CI, p. 248

[W]e have irony as the infinite absolute negativity. It is negativity, because it only negates; it is infinite, because it does not negate this or that phenomenon; it is absolute, because that by virtue of which it negates is a higher something that still is not.

CI, p. 261

In irony, the subject is negatively free, since the actuality that is supposed to give the subject content is not there. . . . But this very freedom, this suspension, gives the ironist a certain enthusiasm, because he becomes intoxicated, so to speak, in the infinity of possibilities . . .

CI, p. 262

Irony is indeed free, free from the sorrows of actuality, but also free from its joys, free from its blessing, for inasmuch as it has nothing higher than itself, it can receive no blessing . . .

CI, p. 279

As the ironist poetically composes himself and his environment with the greatest possible poetic license, as he lives in this totally hypothetical and subjunctive way, his life loses all continuity. He succumbs completely to mood. His life is nothing but moods.

CI, p. 284

There is a lot of talk these days about irony and humor, especially by people who have never been able to practice them but nevertheless know how to explain everything.

FT, p. 51

[W]hat doubt is to science, irony is to personal life.

CI, p. 326

GOD

Father in Heaven! When the thought of you awakens in our soul, let it not awaken like a startled bird which then flutters about in confusion, but like the child from sleep with its heavenly smile.

JN, vol. 1, Journal DD: 189, p. 265

God can just as little prove his existence in any other sense than that in which he is able to swear: he has nothing higher to swear by than himself.

JN, vol. 2, Journal EE: 45, p. 18

It is really remarkable that while all the other attributes ascribed to God are adjectives, "Love" alone is a substantive, and it would scarcely occur to one to make the mistake of saying: ["]God is lovely." Thus language itself has given expression to the substantial element that is found in this attribute.—

JN, vol. 2, Journal EE: 62, p. 22

It is so impossible for the world to exist without God that if God could *forget it*, it would instantly cease to exist.

JN, vol. 2, Journal FF: 54, p. 80

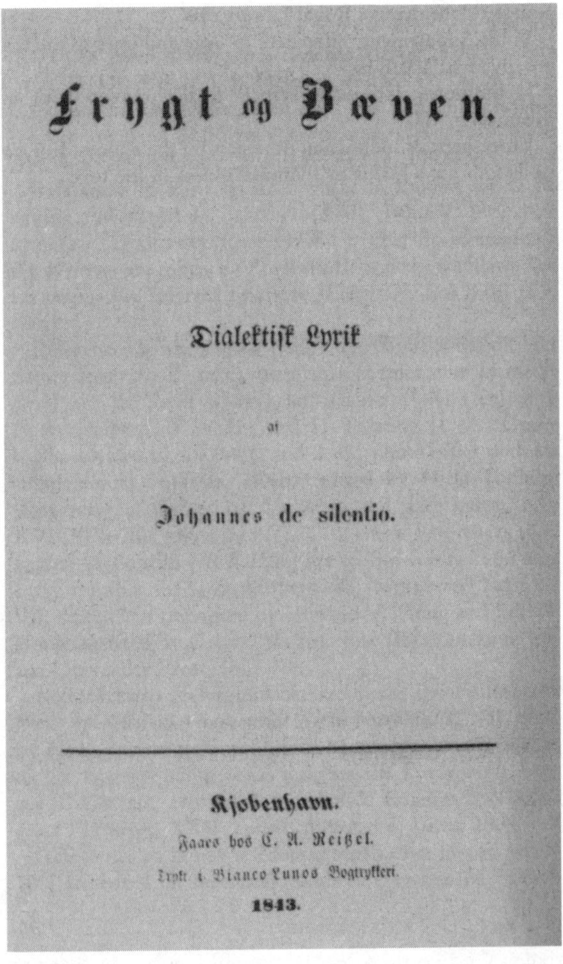

Frygt og Bæven.

Dialektisk Lyrik

af

Johannes de silentio.

Kjøbenhavn.

Faaes hos C. A. Reitzel.

Tryk. i Bianco Lunos Bogtrykkeri.

1843.

FIGURE 13. *Fear and Trembling* title page.

If the subjects in a country in which there was a king enthroned were to sit down to investigate whether it was indeed the best thing to have a king, he would surely be furious. And this is how people behave with respect to God—people forget that God exists and they consider whether it is the best thing, the most satisfactory thing, to have a God.

JN, vol. 2, Journal JJ: 393, p. 251

There are people who say with a certain pride: I owe nothing to any person, I have educated myself. There are others who say: This great thinker was my teacher, this excellent general, and I account it an honor to have been his disciple, to have fought under him—but what would you think if a person were to say: God in heaven was my teacher, and I account it an honor to be his disciple, he brought me up.

JN, vol. 2, Journal JJ: 509, p. 285

There is at once something very humbling and yet infinitely elevating for the individual in the fact that God concerns himself just as much, absolutely just as much, with the least [human being] as with the greatest.

JN, vol. 4, Journal NB: 68, p. 56

Precisely because God cannot be an object for human beings, because God is subject, precisely for this reason the reversal shows itself absolutely: when one denies God—then he does no injury to God but annihilates himself; when one mocks God—then he mocks himself.

JN, vol. 4, Journal NB: 88, p. 73

Imagine a girl who is unhappily in love speaking to a rock about her pain: God listens to your complaint just as impassively, if you imagine that you are the object of his preferential love.

JN, vol. 4, Journal NB: 168, p. 107

I read, somewhere, a very penetrating distinction drawn by Abraham a St. Clara: When a person has withdrawn from the world (in an external sense) but does not live in communion with God—that is, he has the world with him in his thoughts—this person is not solitary; he lives alone but is not solitary.

JN, vol. 4, Journal NB2: 97, p. 178

If the birds do not need to be reminded to praise God, then should not men be moved to prayer without church, in the true house of God, where heaven's arch forms the church ceiling, where the roar of the storm and the gentle zephyr take the place of the organ's bass and treble . . .

JN, vol. 1, Journal AA: 7, p. 12

The divine may well be stirring within earthly relationships and it does not require these to be annihilated as the condition of its appearing, just as God's Spirit revealed itself to Moses in the thornbush, which burned *without being consumed*.

JN, vol. 2, Journal EE: 10, p. 6

All people wish either to be or to become *contemporary* with great men, great events, etc. God knows how many people actually live contemporaneously with themselves. To be contemporary with oneself (thus, not in the feared or expected future or in the past) is transparency in repose, and this is possible only through the relation to God, or it is the relation to God.

JN, vol. 4, Journal NB2: 199, p. 218

The demonstration of the existence of God is something with which one learnedly and metaphysically occupies oneself only on occasion, but the thought of God forces itself upon a man on every occasion.

CA, p. 140

It is an extraordinary benefaction that you came into existence, it is a nice world you came into, and God is a nice fellow; just stay with him, he very likely will not fulfill all your wishes, but he certainly does help. A downright falsehood.

TM, p. 252

It seems as if all this research and pondering and scrutinizing would draw God's Word very close to me; the truth is that this is the very way, this is the most cunning way, to remove God's Word as far as possible from me . . .

FSE, p. 35

When an oak nut is planted in a clay pot, the pot breaks; when new wine is poured into old leather bottles, they burst. What happens, then, when the god plants himself in the frailty of a human being if he does not become a new person and a new vessel!

PF, p. 34

For the fool says in his heart that there is no God, but he who says in his heart or to others: Just wait a little and I shall demonstrate it—ah, what a rare wise man he is!

PF, p. 43

Oh, the true devotion, however, is to give up all claims on life, all claims on power and honor and advantage, all claims—but the happiness of erotic love and friendship is among the very greatest claims—that is, to give up all claims in order to understand what an enormous claim God and eternity have upon the individual himself.

WL, p. 90

Our earthly life, which is frail and infirm, must separate explaining and being, and this weakness of ours is an essential expression of how we relate to God.

WL, p. 101

God is not something external, as is a wife, whom I can ask whether she is now satisfied with me.

CUP, p. 162

Nature, the totality of creation, is God's work, and yet God is not there, but within the individual human being there is a possibility (he is spirit according to his possibility) that in inwardness is awakened to a God-relationship, and then it is possible to see God everywhere.

CUP, pp. 246–47

It by no means follows, however, that a person's life becomes easy because he learns to know God . . .

EUD, p. 324

Only when he himself becomes nothing, only then can God illuminate him so that he resembles God. However great he is, he cannot manifest God's likeness; God can imprint himself in him only when he himself has become nothing. When the ocean is exerting all its power, that is precisely the time when it cannot reflect the image of heaven, and even the slightest motion blurs the image; but when it becomes still and deep, then the image of heaven sinks into its nothingness.

EUD, p. 399

[T]he voice of God is always a whisper . . .

TA, p. 10

In the theater the performance is played before persons present who are called spectators, but at the religious address God himself is present; in the most earnest sense he is the critical spectator who is checking on how it is being spoken and on how it is being heard, and for that very reason there are no spectators. Thus the one speaking is the prompter, and the listener is present and open before God; he is, if I may put it this way, the actor, who in the true sense is acting before God.

UDVS, pp. 124–25

Dependence on God is the only independence . . .
UDVS, p. 182

Among the many goods there is one that is the highest, that is not defined by its relation to the other goods, because it is the highest, and yet the person wishing does not have a definite idea of it, because it is the highest as the unknown—and this good is God.
TDIO, p. 18

Can the Omnipresent One actually have become like a rare natural phenomenon whose existence the scientist demonstrates, or like a variable star observed at century-long intervals and whose existence therefore requires demonstration, especially during the intervening centuries when it is not seen!
TDIO, p. 25

People see God in great things, in the raging of the elements and in the course of world history; they entirely forget what the child understood, that when it shuts its eyes it sees God.
TDIO, p. 31

The person who is without God in the world soon becomes bored with himself—and expresses this haughtily by being bored with all life, but the person who is in fellowship with God indeed lives with the one whose presence gives infinite significance to even the most insignificant.
TDIO, p. 78

The uncharitableness of the natural man cannot allow him the extraordinary that God has intended for him; so he is offended.

SUD, p. 86

God does not avail himself of an abridgment; he comprehends ... actuality itself, all its particulars; for him the single individual does not lie beneath the concept.

SUD, p. 121

The sighing of the wind, the echoing of the forest, the murmuring of the brook, the humming of the summer, the whispering of the leaves, the rustling of the grass, every sound [*Lyd*], every sound you hear is all compliance [*Adlyd*], unconditional obedience [*Lydighed*]. Thus you can hear God in it ...

WA, p. 25

Strangely enough, this deification of the established order is the perpetual revolt, the continual mutiny against God.

PC, p. 88

[T]o God, world history is the royal stage where he, not accidentally but essentially, is the only spectator, because he is the only one who *can* be that. Admission to this theater is not open to any existing spirit. If he fancies himself a spectator there, he is simply forgetting that he himself is supposed to be the actor in that little theater and is to leave it to that royal spectator and poet how he wants to use him in that royal drama, *Drama Dramatum* [The Drama of Dramas].

CUP, p. 158

But you shall love God in unconditional obedience, even if what he requires of you might seem to you to be to your own harm, indeed, harmful to his cause; for God's wisdom is beyond all comparison with yours, and God's governance has no obligation of responsibility in relation to your own sagacity. All you have to do is obey in love.

WL, p. 20

FAITH

It would surely not be unthinkable that a human being could live his entire life constantly worried that he did not have faith, and of whom it might be said—and to whom it would be said: Dear Friend, you had faith, and your worries were only the pains of inwardness.

JN, vol. 2, Journal JJ: 379, p. 246

To have faith is exactly to make oneself light with the aid of considerable gravity to which one subjects oneself; to become objective is to make oneself light by throwing off the burdens. Having faith is just like flying, but one flies precisely with the assistance of a

FIGURE 14. *Fear and Trembling.*
From the Royal Library, Copenhagen, B pk. 10 læg 1.

countervailing gravity; it takes considerable gravity to become light enough to fly.

JN, vol. 4, Journal NB: 65, p. 55

Faith is always related to what is not seen; in the setting of nature (in opposition to the senses) to what is invisible; in the setting of spirit (spiritually) to what is improbable.

JN, vol. 4, Journal NB: 90, p. 74

When one must have a real relation to God, that is, concern oneself with him every day... then one quickly learns that one must make sure to understand that everything God does is good, or learn always to be thankful. Otherwise all that childish nonsense appears: at one moment one is to be thankful, because everything is good or because such and such was so nice; at the next moment one must sigh and beg for patience, because now such and such was so bad. It is impossible to have a real relation to God and at the same time remain in one's merely human and earthly notion of what is of good and bad, pleasant and unpleasant.

JN, vol. 4, Journal NB2: 139, p. 196

Let us rather say it openly, along with honest Kant, who declared the relation to God to be a sort of madness, a hallucination. Being involved with something invisible is of course also like this.

JN, vol. 4, Journal NB2: 235, p. 229

But the Christian knows that to need God is a human being's perfection.

CD, p. 64

An earnest Christian, for example, is well aware that there are moments when he is more profoundly and vitally gripped by the Christian life than he usually is, but he does not therefore become a pagan when the mood passes.

CI, p. 284

[I]f he believes his eyes, he is in fact deceived, for the god cannot be known directly.

PF, p. 63

[A]wareness is by no means partial to faith, as if faith proceeded as a simple consequence of awareness. The advantage is that one enters into a state in which the decision manifests itself ever more clearly.

PF, p. 93

[I]f someone wanted to test whether he has faith, or try to attain faith, this really means he will prevent himself

from attaining faith; he will bring himself into the rest-
lessness of craving where faith is never won . . .

WL, p. 33

Without risk, no faith. Faith is the contradiction between the infinite passion of inwardness and the objective uncertainty.

CUP, p. 204

The believer cares so little for probability that he fears
it most of all, since he knows very well that with it he is
beginning to lose his faith.

CUP, p. 233

Even if someone were able to transpose the whole content of faith into conceptual form, it does not follow
that he has comprehended faith, comprehended how
he entered into it or how it entered into him.

FT, p. 7

But Abraham had faith, and therefore he was young,
for he who always hopes for the best grows old and is
deceived by life, and he who is always prepared for the
worst grows old prematurely, but he who has faith—he
preserves an eternal youth.

FT, p. 18

Love indeed has its priests in the poets, and occasionally we hear a voice that knows how to honor it, but not

a word is heard about faith. Who speaks to the honor of this passion?

FT, p. 32

I wonder if anyone in my generation is able to make the movements of faith?

FT, p. 34

[O]ur generation does not stop with faith, does not stop with the miracle of faith, turning water into wine—it goes further and turns wine into water.

FT, p. 37

The knights of the infinite resignation are easily recognizable—their walk is light and bold. But they who carry the treasure of faith are likely to disappoint, for externally they have a striking resemblance to bourgeois philistinism, which infinite resignation, like faith, deeply disdains.

FT, p. 38

I can still save my soul as long as my concern that my love of God conquer within me is greater than my concern that I achieve earthly happiness.

FT, p. 49

[A]lthough Abraham arouses my admiration, he also appalls me.

FT, p. 60

But faith is the paradox that interiority is higher than exteriority . . .

FT, p. 69

Faith is the highest passion in a person.

FT, p. 122

And this is one of the most decisive definitions for all Christianity—that the opposite of sin is not virtue but faith.

SUD, p. 82

[F]aith conquers the world by conquering at every moment the enemy within one's own inner being, the possibility of offense.

PC, p. 76

Just as the concept "faith" is an altogether distinctively Christian term, so in turn is "offense" an altogether distinctively Christian term relating to faith. The possibility of offense is the crossroad, or it is like standing at the crossroad. From the possibility of offense, one turns either to offense or to faith, but one never comes to faith except from the possibility of offense.

PC, p. 81

If the fear of the Lord is the beginning of wisdom, then learning obedience is the consummation of wisdom . . .

UDVS, p. 258

[T]he believer continually lies out on the deep, has 70,000 fathoms of water beneath him. However long he lies out there, this still does not mean that he will gradually end up lying and relaxing onshore. He can become more calm, more experienced, find a confidence that loves jest and a cheerful temperament—but until the very last he lies out on 70,000 fathoms of water.

SLW, p. 444

It is only all too easy to understand the requirement contained in God's Word ("Give all your goods to the poor." "If anyone strikes you on the right cheek, turn the left." "If anyone takes your coat, let him have your cloak also." "Rejoice always." "Count it sheer joy when you meet various temptations" etc.). It is just as easy to understand as the remark "The weather is fine today," ... The most limited poor creature cannot truthfully deny being able to understand the requirement ...

FSE, pp. 34–35

When the world commences its drastic ordeal, when the storms of life crush youth's exuberant expectancy, when existence, which seemed so affectionate and gentle, changes into a pitiless proprietor who demands everything back, everything that it gave in such a way that it can take it back—then the believer most likely looks at himself and his life with sadness and pain, but he still says, "There is an expectancy that the whole world cannot take from me; it is the expectancy of faith, and this is victory."

EUD, pp. 23–24

PASSION

[P]encil-pushing modern speculative thought takes a dim view of passion, and yet, for the existing person, passion is existence at its very highest—and we are, after all, existing persons.

CUP, p. 197

The passion of the infinite, not its content, is the deciding factor, for its content is precisely itself. In this way the subjective "how" and subjectivity are the truth.

CUP, p. 203

All passion is like sailing: the wind must be sufficiently forceful to stretch the sail with one *uno tenore* [continuous] gust, there must not be too much flapping of the sails and tacking before reaching deep water, there must not be too many preliminaries and prior consultations.

TA, p. 43

Faith is a marvel, and yet no human being is excluded from it; for that which unites all human life is passion, and faith is a passion.

FT, p. 67

[I]t is very easy to leave something behind as a matter of course over the years. And over the years, an individual may abandon the little bit of passion, feeling, imagination, the little bit of inwardness he had and embrace as a matter of course an understanding of life in terms of trivialities . . .

SUD, p. 59

Belief and doubt are not two kinds of knowledge that can be defined in continuity with each other, for neither of them is a cognitive act, and they are opposite passions.

> PF, p. 84

Let others complain that the times are evil. I complain that they are wretched, for they are without passion.

> EO,1, p. 27

Let no one misunderstand all my talk of pathos and passion as if I intended to acknowledge every uncircumcised immediacy, every unshaven passion.

> JN, vol. 2, Journal JJ: 237, p. 199

With respect to what is accidentally unpopular (based on the differences between one human being and another) one has to say that the others don't understand it and that's that. With respect to what is essentially unpopular (to live passionately, absolutely passionately, in something in and for itself) one has to say that the others regard it as lunacy.

> JN, vol. 4, Journal NB5: 142, p. 428

PRAYER

The immediate person believes and fancies that the main thing when he prays, what he is particularly occupied with, is that *God hears* what it is **he** is *praying for*. And yet in the truly eternal sense it is just the opposite: it is not when God hears what is being prayed for that the true prayer relationship occurs but when it *is the one who prays* who continues to pray until it is he *who is the one hearing*, who hears what God wills.

JN, vol. 2, Journal JJ: 464, p. 272

Lord, our God, you know our cares better than we ourselves know them, you know how easily the anxious mind entangles itself in unseasonable and self-made worries, we would pray that you will give us insight to see through their unseasonableness and pride, to scorn them, these busy self-made cares; but the cares you place upon us, we pray that we may humbly accept them from your hand, and that you will give us strength to bear them—

JN, vol. 3, Notebook 5: 16, p. 179

Imagine a girl who is in love—which do you think she loves more: that the beloved, loafing around on a Sunday with nothing to do, happens to remember her and thus to think of her, or that he finds time to think of her even in his busiest moments, albeit without neglecting anything[?] So too, is praying to God in the day of need what he loves best and what is most pleasing to him.

JN, vol. 4, Journal NB5: 13, p. 376

Praying is thus the highest pathos of the infinite, and yet it is comic, precisely because in its inwardness praying is incommensurate with every external expression . . .

    CUP, p. 90

[T]he prayer does not change God, but it changes the one who prays.

    UDVS, p. 22

To pray is also to breathe, and possibility is for the self what oxygen is for breathing.

    SUD, p. 40

EARNESTNESS/SERIOUSNESS*

What is really viewed as seriousness is a certain training, the trained skill in being a husband, a civil servant, etc. If someone spent his time serving the highest idea with enormous diligence, making every sacrifice, or spent his days in dance halls and bars, wasting his fortune: both of these are viewed as equal by these petrified civil servants.

    JN, vol. 4, Journal NB: 53, pp. 48–49

Most people think it is *seriousness* to get an official position, to be attentive to the fact that a higher position,

---

* The Danish term *alvor* can be translated either as "earnestness" or "seriousness."

FIGURE 15. Kierkegaard as a young man.
By Carl Aarsleff. Photograph by Walter Lowrie.

which one can seek, will soon be vacant, and how they will make the move, and what they will then do in order to arrange things. They think it is seriousness to attend distinguished social gatherings; they prepare themselves for a dinner party with His Excellency more than for Holy Communion, and when you see them on the way there, they look so serious that it is quite awful. Look, I can understand all this very well. The only thing I cannot understand is that if this is truly seriousness, then eternity must be sheer fun and games. For in eternity there is neither preferment nor promotion, nor is there a moving day or dinner parties at the homes of Excellencies.

JN, vol. 4, Journal NB: 66, p. 55

Whoever loves can hardly find joy and satisfaction, not to mention growth, in preoccupation with a definition of what love properly is. Whoever lives in daily and festive communion with the thought that there is a God could hardly wish to spoil this for himself, or see it spoiled, by piecing together a definition of what God is. So also with earnestness, which is so earnest a matter that even a definition of it becomes a frivolity.

CA, p. 147

Above all, be an earnest person by having forgotten the one and only earnestness, to relate yourself to God, to become nothing.

WL, p. 103

When someone goes his way bowed low in adversity, sufferings, sickness, lack of appreciation, hardship, and wretched prospects, he draws the wrong conclusion if on the basis of that he directly concludes that he is earnest, because earnestness is not the direct version but the ennobled one . . .

TDIO, p. 74

Earnestness is that you think death, and that you are thinking it is your lot, and that you are then doing what death is indeed unable to do—namely, that you are and death also is.

TDIO, p. 75

No bowstring can be tightened in such a way and is able to give the arrow such momentum the way the thought of death is able to accelerate the living when earnestness stretches the thought.

TDIO, p. 83

Earnestness does not scowl but is reconciled with life and knows how to fear death.

TDIO, p. 88

Ah, my friend, it is far better that you never forget to remember *promptly* than that you promptly say: I will *never* forget it. Earnestness is precisely this kind of honest distrust of oneself, to treat oneself as a suspicious character, as a financier treats an unreliable client, saying, "Well, these big promises are not much help; I would rather have a small part of the total right away."

FSE, p. 44

How consistent life is! There is not anything that is true in one sphere that is not true in another. What profound earnestness that the laws of life are such that everyone must serve them whether he wants to or not.

SLW, p. 384

On the whole ethics has come to be neglected in modern science and scholarship. . . . And that is why ultimately men have forgotten completely what earnestness is and in all earnestness regard as nonsense that which leads to self-knowledge, turns a person out of his delusions, etc.; whereas every communication of knowledge is regarded as earnestness—and yet every communication of knowledge only nourishes the sickness.

JP, vol. 1, no. 649, p. 269

SIN

In the struggle to actualize the task of ethics, sin shows itself not as something that belongs only accidentally to the accidental individual, but as something that withdraws deeper and deeper as a deeper and deeper presupposition, as a presupposition that goes beyond the individual. Then all is lost for ethics . . .

CA, p. 19

Sin is for the ethical consciousness what error is for the knowledge of it—the particular exception that proves nothing.

CA, p. 19

The concept of sin does not properly belong in any science . . .

CA, p. 21

[S]in comes into the world as the sudden, i.e., by a leap . . .

    CA, p. 32

So sinfulness is by no means sensuousness, but without sin there is no sexuality, and without sexuality, no history.

    CA, p. 49

The only thing that is truly able to disarm the sophistry of sin is faith, courage to believe that the state itself is a new sin, courage to renounce anxiety without anxiety, which only faith can do . . .

    CA, p. 117

Let us imagine the greatest criminal who has ever lived and also imagine that by that time physiology will have upon its nose an even more splendid pair of spectacles than ever before, so that it could explain the criminal, explain that the whole thing was a matter of natural necessity, that his brain had been too small, etc. How dreadful is that immunity from all further prosecution in comparison to the judgment Christianity passes on him: that he will go to hell if he does not repent.

    JN, vol. 4, Journal NB: 70, p. 61

Sin is sin; sin is no greater because it is against God or before God. Strange! Even lawyers speak of aggravated crimes; even lawyers make a distinction between a crime committed against a public official, for example, or against a private citizen . . .

    SUD, p. 80

[M]an has to learn what sin is by a revelation from God; sin is not a matter of a person's not having understood what is right but of his being unwilling to understand it . . .

SUD, p. 95

[S]in grows every moment that one does not take leave of it.

SUD, p. 106

The cursory observation that merely looks at the new sin and skips what lies between . . . is just as superficial as supposing that a train moves only when the locomotive puffs.

SUD, p. 106

But the person seeking to understand himself in the consciousness of sin before God does not understand it as a general statement that all people are sinners . . .

TDIO, p. 29

DEMONIC

When one becomes aware of the breadth of the field of the demonic, then perhaps it will also be clear that many of those who want to deal with the phenomenon of the demonic come under the category of the demonic themselves, and that there are traces of it in every man, as surely as every man is a sinner.

CA, p. 122

The demonic is anxiety about the good.

CA, p. 123

An adherent of the most rigid orthodoxy may be demonic. He knows it all. He genuflects before the holy. Truth is for him the aggregate of ceremonies. He talks of meeting before the throne of God and knows how many times one should bow. He knows everything, like the man who can prove a mathematical proposition when the letters are ABC, but not when the letters are DEF.

CA, pp. 139–40

Sin itself is a struggle of despair; but then, when all the powers are depleted, there may be a new intensification, a new demonic closing up within himself: this is despair over sin.

SUD, p. 110

[T]his is the deep contradiction in the demonic, and in a certain sense there is ever so much more good in a demoniac than in superficial people.

FT, p. 96

The demonic has the same quality as the divine, namely, that the single individual is able to enter into an absolute relation to it.

FT, p. 97

REPENTANCE/FORGIVENESS

A person reposes in the forgiveness of sins when the thought of God no longer reminds him of the sin, but of the fact that it is forgiven, so that what is past is not a recollection of how much he offended, but of how much he has been forgiven.

JN, vol. 4, Journal NB2: 116, p. 185

It was a miracle when Christ said to the paralyzed man: Your sins are forgiven, stand up and walk. Though this miracle has not happened to me—what miraculous confidence and openness in faith to believe that sin is completely forgotten so that no anxiety accompanies one's memory of it; truly to believe that one has become a new person so that one scarcely recognizes oneself.

JN, vol. 4, Journal NB4: 156, p. 360

But there is also a love with which I love God, and this love has only one expression in language—it is "repentance." If I do not love him in this way, then I do not love him absolutely, out of my innermost being.

EO,2, p. 216

Repentance specifically expresses that evil essentially belongs to me and at the same time expresses that it does not essentially belong to me.

EO,2, p. 224

FIGURE 16. Gammeltorv.
Lithograph by Em. Baerentzen. From a photograph
in the Picture Collection of the Royal Library.
Reproduced courtesy of the Royal Library.

Sin advances in its consequence; repentance follows it step by step, but always a moment too late.

CA, p. 115

But without honesty there is no repentance. . . . To repent of a generality without substance is a contradiction . . .

TDIO, pp. 34–35

One can indeed forget in many ways. One can forget because one gets something else to think about; one can forget thoughtlessly and light-mindedly; one can think that everything is forgotten because one has oneself forgotten. But eternal justice can and will forget in only one way, through forgiveness—but then, of course, the believer must not forget either, but he must steadfastly recollect that it is forgiven him.

UDVS, p. 247

Just as one by faith *believes* the *unseen into* what is seen, so the one who loves by forgiveness *believes away* what is seen. Both are faith. Blessed is the believer, he believers what he cannot see; blessed is the one who loves, he believes away that which he indeed can see!

WL, p. 295

CHRIST

One rants so much against anthropomorphisms and fails to remember that the birth of Christ is the greatest and most meaningful.

JN, vol. 1, Journal DD: 34, p. 225

What precisely is profound in Christianity is that Christ is both our atoner and our judge, not that one is our atoner and another our judge, for then we would nevertheless come to be judged, but that the atoner and the judge are the same.

JN, vol. 1, Journal DD: 142, p. 253

Christ did not concern himself with writing—he wrote only in sand.

JN, vol. 2, Journal FF: 105, p. 88

Present-day Christendom really lives as if the situation were as follows: Christ is the great hero and benefactor who has once and for all secured salvation for us; now we must merely be happy and delighted with the innocent goods of earthly life and leave the rest to him. But Christ is essentially the exemplar, that is, we are to *resemble* him, not merely profit from him.

JN, vol. 4, Journal NB2: 182, p. 212

But didn't Christ come into the world to take suffering away, so that we should be happy—not to bring new sufferings[?] Doesn't taking it this way make his whole coming into the world futile? On the contrary. He came into the world to transform humanity in such a way that all these human sufferings (poverty, penury, sickness, loss of honor, etc.) become as something childish, something to be reckoned as nothing.

JN, vol. 4, NB5: 143, p. 428

With Christ as the Exemplar, what we human beings might call intellectuality is not at all prominent. That is why we would find it offensive to think of Christ laughing, something that is expressed in the hymn: Why does he cry, who never laughed[?]

JN, vol. 6, Journal NB12: 128, p. 221

Christ was the fulfilling of the Law. How this thought is to be understood we are to learn from him, because he was *the explanation*, and only when the explanation *is* what it explains, when the explainer *is* what is explained, when the explanation [*Forklaring*] is the transfiguration [*Forklarelse*], only then is the relation the right one.

WL, p. 101

In Christ everything is revealed—and *everything* is hidden.

EUD, p. 433

If Christ is proclaimed to you, then it is offense to say: I do not want to have any opinion about it.

SUD, p. 129

What ungodly thoughtlessness that makes sacred history into profane history, Christ into a human being! Can one, then, come to know something about Jesus Christ from history? By no means. Jesus Christ is the object of faith; one must either believe in him or be offended; for to "know" simply means that it is not about him.

PC, p. 33

If one has only a fantastic picture of Christ, if he is not the individual human being who stands face to face with one, and his father, the carpenter, is not an actual individual human being with whom one is well acquainted, and likewise the rest of his relatives—then it is quite possible not to be offended. But if one is not contemporary with Christ in this way, then it is also impossible to become Christian.

PC, p. 103

LOVE

They say love makes one blind; it does more than that, it makes one deaf, it paralyses one; the person suffering from it is like the mimosa that closes so no picklock can open it; the more force one uses, the more tightly is it shut.

JN, vol. 3, Notebook 8: 11, p. 223

Does not even an otherwise humble gift, an insignificant little something, have infinite worth for the lover when it is from the beloved!

    CD, p. 15

Being in love is the culmination of a person's purely human existence, which is a double existence, and for that very reason being in love is simultaneously just as much inwardness as it is a relation directed outwardly to actuality.

    TA, p. 49

There has been much talk in the world about unhappy love, and everyone knows what the term means: that the lovers are unable to have each other. And the reasons—well, there can be a host of them. There is another kind of unhappy love: the love of which we speak, to which there is no perfect earthly analogy but which we nevertheless, by speaking loosely for a while, can imagine in an earthly setting. The unhappiness is the result not of the lovers' being unable to have each other but of their being unable to understand each other. And this sorrow is indeed infinitely deeper than the sorrow of which people speak, for this unhappiness aims at the heart of love and wounds for eternity . . .

    PF, pp. 25–26

What is it, namely, that connects the temporal and eternity, what else but love, which for that very reason is before everything and remains after everything is gone.

    WL, p. 6

Love's hidden life is in the innermost being, unfathomable, and then in turn is in an unfathomable connectedness with all existence.

WL, p. 9

In other words, just as love itself is invisible and therefore we have to believe in it, so also is it not unconditionally and directly to be known by any particular expression of it.

WL, p. 13

There is no word in human language, not one single one, not the most sacred one, about which we are able to say: If a person uses this word, it is unconditionally demonstrated that there is love in that person. On the contrary, it is even true that a word from one person can convince us that there is love in him, and the opposite word from another can convince us that there is love in him also. It is true that one and the same word can convince us that love abides in the one who said it and does not in the other, who nevertheless said the same word.

WL, p. 13

But the one who is busily occupied tracking down hypocrites, whether he succeeds or not, had better see to it that this is not also a hypocrisy, inasmuch as such discoveries are hardly the fruits of love.

WL, p. 15

The best defense against hypocrisy is love . . .

WL, p. 15

If mistrust can actually see something as less than it is, then love also can see something as greater than it is.

WL, p. 16

Christianity certainly knows far better than any poet what love is and what it means to love. For this very reason it also knows what perhaps escapes the poets, that the love they celebrate is secretly self-love, and that precisely by this its intoxicated expression—to love another person more than oneself—can be explained.

WL, p. 19

The commandment said, "You shall love your neighbor as yourself," but if the commandment is properly understood it also says the opposite: *You shall love yourself in the right way.*

WL, p. 22

Whoever has any knowledge of people will certainly admit that just as he has often wished to be able to move them to relinquish self-love, he has also had to wish that it were possible to teach them to love themselves.

WL, p. 23

Consequently, *only when it is a duty to love, only then is love eternally secured.* The security of eternity casts out all anxiety and makes love perfect, perfectly secured.

WL, p. 32

Is changingness indeed a stronger power than changelessness, and who is the stronger, the one who says, "If you will not love me, then I will hate you," or the one who says, "If you hate me, I will still continue to love you"?

WL, p. 34

The jealous person catches, almost imploringly, every beam from the love in the beloved, but through the burning glass of jealousy he focuses all these beams on his own love, and he slowly burns up.

WL, p. 35

If, however, love has undergone eternity's change by becoming duty, it does not know habit and habit can never gain power over it. Just as eternal life is said to have no sighing and no tears, so one could add: and no habit either, and truly by this we do not say anything less glorious.

WL, p. 37

People think that it is impossible for a human being to love his enemy, because, alas, enemies are hardly able to endure the sight of one another. Well, then, shut your eyes—then the enemy looks just like the neighbor. Shut your eyes and remember the commandment that *you* shall love; then you love—your enemy—no, then you love the neighbor, because you do not see that he is your enemy.

WL, p. 68

Moreover, learn and never forget the lesson, this sadness that is the truth of earthly life, that all love between human beings neither can be nor will be perfectly happy, never dares to be perfectly secure! In the divine sense, even the happiest love between two people still has one danger that the merely human view of love does not think of, the danger that the earthly love could become too intense, so that the God–relationship is disturbed . . .

WL, p. 129

But to love oneself in the divine sense is to love God, and truly to love another person is to help that person to love God or in loving God.

WL, p. 130

When it is a duty to love the people we see, *one must first and foremost give up all imaginary and exaggerated ideas about a dreamworld where the object of love should be sought and found—that is, one must become sober, gain actuality and truth by finding and remaining in the world of actuality as the task assigned to one.*

WL, p. 161

Therefore if you want to be perfect in love, strive to fulfill this duty, in loving to love the person one sees, to love him just as you see him, with all his imperfections and weaknesses, to love him as you see him when he has changed completely, when he no longer loves you but perhaps turns away indifferent or turns away to love another, to love him as you see him when he betrays and denies you.

WL, p. 174

Love, on the other hand—oh, it is not like an art, jealous of itself and therefore bestowed on only a few. Everyone who wants to have love is given it, and if he wants to undertake the task of praising it, he will succeed in that also.

WL, p. 360

Much that is said praising a mother's love for her child is, of course, rooted in a misunderstanding, since maternal love as such is simply self-love raised to a higher power, and thus the animals also have it. That this kind of love in its initial state is self-love is apparent . . .

WL, p. 483

Love for God and love for neighbor are like two doors that open simultaneously, so that it is impossible to open one without also opening the other, and impossible to shut one without also shutting the other.

WL, p. 487

But the person who can scarcely open himself cannot love, and the person who cannot love is the unhappiest of all.

EO,2, p. 160

Alas, how utterly different married life and marriage conditions are in this world, and yet there is one resolution common to each and every one or can be so: that love [*Kjerlighed*] conquers everything.

TDIO, p. 67

But the true expression of loving much is just to forget oneself completely. If one remembers oneself, one can, to be sure, love but not love much; and the more one remembers oneself, to the same degree one loves less.

WA, p. 140

No one who was great in the world will be forgotten, but everyone was great in his own way, and everyone in proportion to the greatness of that which *he loved*. He who loved himself became great by virtue of himself, and he who loved other men became great by his devotedness, but he who loved God became the greatest of all.

FT, p. 16

The person who truly loves does not love once for all; neither does he use a portion of his love now and then in turn another portion . . . No, he loves with all his love; it is totally present in every expression; he continually spends all of it, and yet he continually keeps it all in his heart. What marvelous wealth!

UDVS, p. 30

I do not have the right to become insensitive to life's pain, because I *shall* sorrow; but neither do I have the right to despair, because I shall sorrow; and neither do I have the right to stop sorrowing, because I *shall* sorrow. So it is with love. You do not have the right to become insensitive to this feeling, because you *shall* love; but neither do you have the right to love despairingly, because you *shall* love; and just as little do you have the right to warp this feeling in you, because you *shall* love.

WL, p. 43

Worldly wisdom is of the opinion that love is a relationship between persons; Christianity teaches that love is a relationship between: a person—God—a person, that is, that God is the middle term.

WL, pp. 106–7

SUFFERING

It is and remains the most difficult spiritual trial when a person doesn't know whether insanity or sin is the reason for his suffering. Here freedom, otherwise used as the means with which to fight, has become dialectical with its dreadful contrasts.

JN, vol. 2, Journal JJ: 242, p. 200

Suffering patiently is not at all specifically Christian—but freely choosing suffering from which one could escape, freely choosing it for the sake of a good cause: that is Christian.

JN, vol. 4, Journal NB2: 145, p. 199

At its deepest level, all offense is a suffering.

PF, p. 49

There is so much talk about human distress and wretchedness—I try to understand it and have also had some intimate acquaintance with it—there is so much talk about wasting a life, but only that person's life was wasted who went on living so deceived by life's joys or its sorrows that he never became decisively and eternally conscious as spirit, as self . . .

SUD, p. 26

NEIGHBOR

Think of the most cultured person, one of whom we all admiringly say, "He is so cultured!" Then think of Christianity, which says to him, "You shall love the neighbor!" Of course, a certain social courtesy, a politeness toward all people, a friendly condescension toward inferiors, a boldly confident attitude before the mighty, a beautifully controlled freedom of spirit, yes, this is culture—do you believe that it is also loving the neighbor?

WL, p. 60

The neighbor is one who is equal. The neighbor is neither the beloved, for whom you have passion's preference, nor your friend, for whom you have passion's preference.

WL, p. 60

The neighbor is every person, since on the basis of dissimilarity he is not your neighbor, nor on the basis of similarity to you in your dissimilarity from other people.

WL, p. 60

At a distance the neighbor is a shadow that walks past everyone's thoughts on the road of imagination, but that the person who actually walked by at the same moment was the neighbor—this he perhaps does not discover.

WL, p. 79

Take many sheets of paper, write something different on each one; then no one will be like another. But then again take each single sheet; do not let yourself be confused by the diverse inscriptions, hold it up to the light, and you will see a common watermark on all of them. In the same way the neighbor is the common watermark, but you see it only by means of eternity's light when it shines through the dissimilarity.

WL, p. 89

If everyone in truth loved the neighbor as himself, then perfect human equality would be achieved unconditionally.

PV, p. 111

One has no neighbor; for the "I" is at once itself and its neighbor, as also it is expressed: One is closest to oneself (i.e., one's own neighbor).

JN, vol. 1, Journal DD: 32a, p. 225

What Socrates says about loving the ugly is really the Christian teaching concerning love of neighbor.

JN, vol. 4, Journal NB2: 77, p. 171

One must really have suffered very much in the world, have become very unhappy, before there can be any talk whatsoever of beginning to love one's neighbor. Only in self-denial's dying-away from earthly delight and happiness and happy days, only then does "the neighbor" come into existence. . . . Everyone who clings to earthly life does not love his neighbor, that is, his neighbor does not exist for him.

JN, vol. 4, Journal NB2: 155, p. 201

Deep down, many people think that the Christian commandments (e.g., loving your neighbor as yourself), are deliberately made a little bit too rigorous—rather as when the clock that serves to wake the household is 1/2 an hour too fast in order that one doesn't get up too late in the morning.

JN, vol. 4, Journal NB5: 26, p. 381

CHRISTIANITY

There is so much talk about how Christianity presupposes nothing at all on the part of the human being, [but] it obviously presupposes one thing: that is, *self-love*, for Christ obviously presupposes it when he says

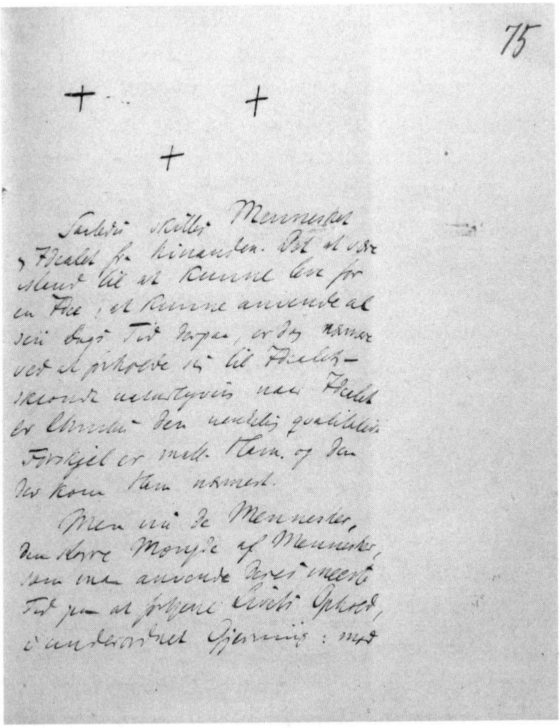

FIGURE 17. Journal entry.
Source: JN, vol. 5, Journal NB10: 57, p. 297.

that love of the neighbor is to be as great as love toward ourselves.

JN, vol. 2, Journal EE: 98, p. 32

The consciousness of sin is and remains *conditio sine qua non* for all Christianity . . .

JN, vol. 2, Journal JJ: 205, p. 189

As long as a person has many wells from which to draw water, he is not aware of having any anxious concerns about the possible unavailability of water. But when a person has only one single well! And thus it is only when Christianity becomes the sole well for a person that spiritual trials begin.

JN, vol. 4, Journal NB: 159, p. 104

Oh, but how shamefully people have even made use of Christianity in order to refine what is worldly. Someone desires worldly things more than does any pagan—but in addition cloaks it with Christian disdain for everything worldly. Thank you, this is harvesting twice.

JN, vol. 6, Journal NB12: 59, p. 174

Ah, there is indeed something sadly true in the circumstance that it would be better that Christianity not be preached at all than that it be preached as it is nowadays. To be elated for an hour in this way once a week just as one is in the theater, and then the problem is exactly that one gets accustomed to hearing everything without it in any way occurring to a person that he do something.

JN, vol. 6, Journal NB12: 151, p. 239

In the magnificent palace church, a handsome court preacher, the cultivated public's chosen one, steps before a select circle of the distinguished and cultured, and preaches movingly on the words of the apostle, ["]God chose the lowly and the despised["]—and no one laughs.

JN, vol. 6, Journal NB14: 53, p. 380

And the day when Christianity and the world become friends—yes, then Christianity is abolished.

PC, p. 224

The Christian truth has, if I may say so, its own eyes with which to see; indeed, it seems to be all eyes. But it would be very disturbing, indeed, it would be impossible, for me to look at a painting or a piece of cloth if I discovered while looking at it that it was the painting or the cloth that was looking at me. And this is the case with the Christian truth ∴ .

PC, p. 234

There is something that God cannot take away from a human being, namely, the voluntary, and it is precisely this that Christianity requires.

CD, p. 179

Truly, there is something that is more against Christianity and the essence of Christianity than any heresy, any schism, more against it than all heresies and schisms together, and it is this: to play at Christianity.

TM, p. 6

"Grace" cannot possibly stretch so far; one thing it must never be used for—it must never be used to suppress or to diminish the requirement. In that case "grace" turns all Christianity upside down.

TM, p. 47

Christianity did not enter into the world in order to reassure you in your natural condition (thus assuring the pastor a thriving and pleasant livelihood), but that it, renouncing all things, entered into the world in order, with the terrors of eternity, to wrest you out of the peace in which you naturally are.

TM, p. 312

A Christian is a person who has caught on fire.

TM, p. 465

Christianity is the only historical phenomenon that despite the historical—indeed, precisely by means of the historical—has wanted to be the single individual's point of departure for his eternal consciousness, has wanted to interest him otherwise than merely historically, has wanted to base his happiness on his relation to something historical.

PF, p. 109

Although an outsider, I have at least understood this much, that the only unforgivable high treason against Christianity is the single individual's taking his relation to it for granted.

CUP, p. 16

In those early days, a Christian was a fool in the eyes of the world. To the pagans and Jews it was foolishness for him to want to become one. Now one is a Christian as a matter of course. If someone wants to be a Christian with infinite passion, he is a fool . . .

CUP, p. 216

What I recoil from, then, even more than from dying or from losing my dearest treasure, is to say of Christianity that is true to a certain degree.

CUP, p. 234

[I]f Christianity were a doctrine, then the relation to it would not be one of faith, since there is only an intellectual relation to a doctrine. Christianity, therefore, is not a doctrine but the fact that the god has existed.

CUP, p. 326

That one can know what Christianity is without being a Christian must, then, be answered in the affirmative. Whether one can know what it is to be a Christian without being one is something else, and it must be answered in the negative.

CUP, p. 372

If one were to state and describe in a single sentence the victory Christianity has won over the world or, even more correctly, the victory by which it has more than overcome the world . . . then I know of nothing shorter but also nothing more decisive than this: it has made every human relationship between person and person a relationship of conscience.

WL, p. 135

Christianity does not want to make changes in externals; neither does it want to abolish drives or inclination—it wants only to make infinity's change in the inner being.

WL, p. 139

Humanly speaking, death is the last of all, and, humanly speaking, there is hope only as long as there is life. Christianly understood, however, death is by no means the last of all; in fact, it is only a minor event within that which is all, an eternal life . . .

SUD, p. 7

Christianity thinks that it is the unconditioned, and that alone, or the impression, the impact of the unconditioned, that is able to make a person completely sober when he unconditionally surrenders to its power, and otherwise he has not felt the impact of the unconditioned; that on the other hand it is precisely this "to a certain degree" that is intoxicating and stupefying, makes one heavy, drowsy, sluggish, and apathetic, somewhat like an alcoholic, who is said to walk around in a continual stupor.

FSE, pp. 106–7

[O]h, that I had a voice that could be heard, and would that I could give it significance like that of a dying person's voice, and that what I said could continue to sound, because it is so crucial!—in possibility Christianity is easy; and merely expounded, that is, kept in possibility, it pleases people. In actuality it is so difficult, and expressed in actuality, that is, as action, it incites people against you.

FSE, pp. 116–17

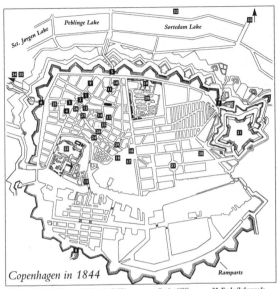

1. University of Copenhagen
2. Church of Our Lady
3. Gammeltorv
4. Nytorv
 [Kierkegaard lived at
 Nytorv 2, now torn down,
 until September 1837, and
 from October 1844 to
 April 1848]
5. Nørreport
6. Vesterport
7. Østerport
8. Amagerport
9. Nørregade
 [Kierkegaard lived at
 Nørregade 230A, now no.
 38, from April/October
 1840 to October 1844, and
 at Nørregade 43, now no.

35, from April 1850 to
April 1851]
10. Rosenborggade
 [Kierkegaard lived at
 Rosenborggade 156A,
 now no. 9, from April
 1848 to April 1850]
11. Kultorvet
 [Kierkegaard lived at
 Kultorvet 132, now no. 11,
 from late 1839/early 1840
 to April/October 1840]
12. Klædeboderne
 [Kierkegaard lived at
 Klædeboderne 5–6, now
 Skindergade 38/Dyrkøb
 5 (he lived on the Dyrkøb
 side, with a view of the
 Church of Our Lady),
 from April/October 1852

to October 1855]
13. Borgerdyd School
14. Løvstræde
 [Kierkegaard lived at
 Løvstræde 7 (the probable
 location; it is now torn
 down) from September
 1837 to ca. June 1838]
15. Olsen family home
16. Kongens Nytorv
17. Charlottenborg
18. Royal Theater
19. Rosenborg Castle
20. Royal Gardens
21. Amalienborg Castle
22. Christiansborg Castle
23. Købmagergade
24. Højbro Plads

25. Frederiksberggade
26. Nygade
27. Vimmelskaftet
28. Amagertorv
29. Østergade
30. Frederik's Hospital
31. Citadel
32. Blegdamsvej
33. Østerbro
 [Kierkegaard lived at
 Østerbro 108A (at the site
 where Willemoesgade
 enters Østerbrogade; it is
 now torn down) from
 April 1851 to April/
 October 1852]
34. Hill House
 [Bakkehus]
35. Frederiksberg Gardens

FIGURE 18. Map of Copenhagen.
Source: Kirmmse, *Encounters with Kierkegaard*, p. xv.

Soon it will have gone so far that an admirer of Christianity is a rarity; the average person is lukewarm, neither cold nor hot, and many are atheists, mockers, nonreligious persons, deniers. But in the strictest sense "the admirer" is still not a true Christian; if it cannot be said that he is lukewarm because there is heat in him, neither can it be said that he is hot. Only the imitator is the true Christian.

PC, p. 256

The established order continues to stand, but since it is equivocal and ambiguous, passionless reflection is reassured. We do not want to abolish the monarchy, by no means, but if little by little we could get it transformed into make-believe, we would gladly shout "Hurrah for the King!" We do not want to topple eminence, by no means, but if simultaneously we could spread the notion that it is all make-believe, we would approve and admire. . . . [W]e are willing to keep Christian terminology but privately know that nothing decisive is supposed to be meant by it.

TA, pp. 80–81

BIBLIOGRAPHY

Cappelørn, Niels Jørgen, Joakim Garff, and Johnny Kondrup. *Written Images*. Translated by Bruce H. Kirmmse. Princeton University Press, 1997.

Evans, C. Stephen. *Kierkegaard: An Introduction*. Cambridge University Press, 2009.

Garff, Joachim. *Søren Kierkegaard: A Biography*. Translated by Bruce H. Kirmmse. Princeton University Press, 2007.

Gouwens, David J. *Kierkegaard as Religious Thinker*. Cambridge University Press, 1996.

Hannay, Alastair. *Kierkegaard*. Routledge & Kegan Paul, 1982.

———. *Kierkegaard: A Biography*. Cambridge University Press, 2003.

Hannay, Alastair, and Gordon D. Marino (eds.). *The Cambridge Companion to Kierkegaard*. Cambridge University Press, 1997.

Kirmmse, Bruce H., ed. *Encounters with Kierkegaard: A Life as Seen by His Contemporaries*. Translated by Bruce H. Kirmmse and V. R. Laursen. Princeton University Press, 1996.

———. *Kierkegaard in Golden Age Denmark*. Indiana University Press, 1990.

LeFevre, Perry D. (ed.). *The Prayers of Kierkegaard.* University of Chicago Press, 1996.

Lippitt, John, and George Pattison (eds.). *The Oxford Handbook of Kierkegaard.* Oxford University Press, 2013.

Lowrie, Walter. *Kierkegaard.* Oxford University Press, 1938.

———. *A Short Life of Kierkegaard.* 1938. Reissue, Princeton University Press, 2013.

Malantschuk, Gregor. *Kierkegaard's Thought.* Translated by Howard V. and Edna H. Hong. Princeton University Press, 1972.

Oden, Thomas C. (ed.). *Parables of Kierkegaard.* Princeton University Press, 1989.

——— (ed.). *The Humor of Kierkegaard: An Anthology.* Princeton University Press, 2004.

Watkin, Julia. *Historical Dictionary of Kierkegaard's Philosophy.* Scarecrow Press, 2001.

INDEX

Note: Page numbers in italic type indicate illustrations.